*Adventures
in Spiritual Warfare*

Adventures in Spiritual Warfare

Defeating Satan and Living a Victorious Life

William P. Payne

Foreword by
Charles H. Kraft

RESOURCE *Publications* • Eugene, Oregon

ADVENTURES IN SPIRITUAL WARFARE
Defeating Satan and Living a Victorious Life

Copyright © 2018 William P. Payne. All rights reserved. Except for brief quotations in critical publications or reviews, no part of this book may be reproduced in any manner without prior written permission from the publisher. Write: Permissions, Wipf and Stock Publishers, 199 W. 8th Ave., Suite 3, Eugene, OR 97401.

Resource Publications
An Imprint of Wipf and Stock Publishers
199 W. 8th Ave., Suite 3
Eugene, OR 97401

www.wipfandstock.com

PAPERBACK ISBN: 978-1-5326-4401-6
HARDCOVER ISBN: 978-1-5326-4402-3
EBOOK ISBN: 978-1-5326-4403-0

Manufactured in the U.S.A.

Copyright 2018 William P. Payne. All rights reserved. Except for brief quotations in critical publications or reviews, no part of this book may be reproduced in any manner without the written permission from the publisher. Write: Permissions, Wipf and Stock Publishers, 199 W. 8th Ave., Suite 3, Eugene, OR 97401.

Scripture quotations marked (NIV) are taken from the Holy Bible, New International Version®, NIV®. Copyright © 1973, 1978, 1984, 2011 by Biblica, Inc.™ Used by permission of Zondervan. All rights reserved worldwide. www.zondervan.com The "NIV" and "New International Version" are trademarks registered in the United States Patent and Trademark Office by Biblica, Inc.™

For my wife, Ann, all those who have patiently mentored me and encouraged me along the way.

Contents

Foreword by Charles H. Kraft | xi
Introduction | xiii

Section One: What I Didn't Learn in Seminary

Chapter 1 Antecedents: Shadows of a Looming Darkness | 3
    A Haunted Barracks in Okinawa
    The Strange Case of the Man in a Fetal Position
    A Woman Suffering from Post-Abortion Stress Syndrome

Chapter 2 Engaging the Battle | 12
    My House Is Haunted
    Closing the Loop on Missing Things

Chapter 3 Dark Tide Rising | 19
    Breaking Demonic Associations
    Problems with Sex Spirits
    Are Sex Demons Real?
    An Unfortunate Encounter with a Witch
    Personal Attacks
    More Audacious Attacks
    Learning to Surrender to God

Section Two: Spiritually Equipped for Anointed Ministry

Chapter 4 The Disciples Are Equipped to Do Anointed Ministry | 37
    Trained to Do Power Ministry
    Jesus Needed Spirit-Baptism
    The Disciples Are Spirit-filled So They Can Accomplish the Mission of God

Contents

Chapter 5 Gifted for Mission and Ministry | 45
    Old Testament Examples of People Being Filled with the Spirit for Special Tasks
    The Night I Spoke in Tongues
    The Night My Youth Minister Spoke in Tongues
    Global Pentecostalism

Chapter 6 Flowing with Spiritual Gifts | 54
    Learning How to Flow with the Spirit
    A Student Discovers a Gift
    The Example of Jesus and Spiritual Gifts
    How to Discern Your Gifting

Section Three: Defeating Demons

Chapter 7 Overcoming the Enemy When Demons Appear | 63
    Demons Oppose Evangelism
    Confronted by Angry Demons in Latin America
    More Demon Stories
    A Sleepy Demon
    A Spirit of Insanity
    Both/And Thinking
    A Muslim Comes to Faith in My Evangelism Class
    Stirring Up Demons through Anointed Preaching
    Expect the Unexpected

Chapter 8 How the Demonic Manipulates Soul-Ties | 84
    What Are Soul-Ties?
    The Mother/Child Soul-Tie
    Manipulating Emotional Links
    Forming Temporary Emotional Ties
    Can Demons Move through Soul-Ties?

Chapter 9 Secondhand Smoke | 93
    Joan's Story
    Soul-Ties and the Family Unit

CONTENTS

Chapter 10 Fire Ants and Demons: Knowing Our God-Given Dominion | 99
    Claiming Our Dominion
    Walking under the Covering of God's Protection
    Establishing a Cover
    A Haunted Curve in the Trail

Section Four: Spiritual Gifts Enable Spiritual Warfare

Chapter 11 Dimensions of Healing | 111
    Demons that Cause Illness
    The Evil Eye

Chapter 12 Using Words of Knowledge in Ministry | 116
    Personal Examples
    Esperanza: The Day God Gave Me Hope
    Receiving Knowledge through Dreams and Visions

Chapter 13 Raising the Dead Is Spiritual Warfare | 125
    Raising the Dead Is More Common Than You Think
    Why Do Bad Things Happen to Good People?
    Joseph's Story
    Prevailing Prayer
    The Outcome of Prevailing Prayer
    Conclusion

Bibliography | 135

Foreword

OUR ENEMY, SATAN, is alive and well and very active. Yet we in the sophisticated West go along merrily assuming that he doesn't exist, except in fairy tales. We even explain away biblical references to Jesus' dealing with "demons" as "primitive" attempts to explain psychological phenomena.

And our enemy laughs at our self-imposed blindness and goes ahead with his schemes to influence us and our institutions without being recognized. We often see the results of Satan's activity but interpret them as purely human.

Until something happens that doesn't fit into our paradigm and we're forced to either ignore the event or to consider an interpretation from outside our worldview.

Most of the time our enemy stays nicely hidden. But sometimes he does things in such a way that only the most skeptical can ignore that something is going on outside the reality in which we live.

Bill Payne was blasted out of his comfort zone through exposure to a number of experiences that didn't fit into his comfortable paradigms. This book, like the Bible, is a casebook of those experiences, challenging us to believe in and recognize that there is a spirit world that interacts with our familiar material world and needs to be taken seriously.

Read this book and make the changes in your worldview if you haven't already done so. Note the reality of evil spirits and who wins when they are confronted by someone working in the power of God. The power Jesus gives us is infinitely greater than the power of the enemy. Freedom is the prize

Foreword

I pray that you will join Jesus in this war and experience the victory that Bill has done such a good job of demonstrating.

Charles H. Kraft, PhD.,
Professor Emeritus of Anthropology and Intercultural Communication at Fuller School of Intercultural Studies (formerly School of World Mission) in Pasadena, CA.

Introduction

In 2003, a tsunami of evil supernaturalism crashed against my home. The ensuing havoc disrupted my family's equilibrium and permanently altered our window into reality. Unlike a benign episode of "Ghost Hunters" in which excited people think they hear whispers as they chase after ephemeral shadows, my family grappled with a substantive haunting. To put it bluntly, we experienced the type of events that you see in horror movies or read about in science fiction novels. The first wave of attacks lasted for three months. Subsequent waves of bizarre and brazen incursions punctuated the following years.

At first, I discussed the overt phenomena in quiet undertones because I felt embarrassed to talk about spiritual attacks in open conversation. After all, how does a respected professor talk to his neighbors, colleagues, students, and friends about paranormal activity? In any case, the *Diagnostic and Statistical Manual of Mental Disorders*[1] has a category for "delusional disorders." I didn't want to be that person.

Soon, I discovered a group of fellow travelers, trusted companions with whom I could confide my struggles and share what I was learning. On one occasion, a confidant bemused that I attracted demons like Lee Trevino's golf clubs attracted lightning.[2] Another nicknamed me "demon rod" (a play on "lightning rod"). Call it paranoia. I couldn't argue with the assessment.

Things reached a crescendo in 2014. In April, while in the midst of a protracted and challenging period of intense spiritual warfare, I posted the following status on Facebook.

---

1. American Psychiatric Association. *Diagnostic and Statistical Manual of Mental Disorders DSM-5*.

2. The odds of being hit by lightning in your lifetime are one in 300,000. PGA golfer, Lee Trevino has been struck by lightning three times.

INTRODUCTION

> About four weeks ago, evil supernaturalism unleashed a virulent, multivalent attack. Friends and colleagues who have joined with me to pray against the evil powers of wickedness have also been aggressed in spiritual and physical ways. Some feel shaken and a bit confused. Still, we have regrouped and have launched a spiritual counterattack. As we prayed together last Friday, I sensed a deep yearning for revival. Nothing threatens Satan's hegemony more than united cries for revival. God has given me peace and a growing sense of expectation even amidst this time of turmoil.
>
> Sadly, a few battle-weary saints have adopted a defeatist strategy of laying low hoping to avoid the enemy's notice. Considering what we have endured, I don't call this cowardice. Still, I know that the Evil One wants us to hide, disengage, and retreat from the battle. In the face of this intractable adversary, we must not yield to fear or to his intimidation. For we are not unaware of the devil's schemes (2 Cor 2:11). Now is the time for the united saints to advance the cause of God. Now is the time for us to take the battle directly to the spiritual forces of wickedness that have sought to put us and our city in bondage.
>
> Mark my words. God is up to something and the devil wants to stop it! His intense and flagrant hostility shows that our warfare prayers are pulling down his strongholds. I believe that we are on the cusp of a massive breakthrough, a breakthrough that will usher in a time of renewal and victory.

Life hasn't gone back to normal. Since the first attack in 2003, one adventure has led to another. The incessant nature of my frequent encounters with the "dark side" has forced me to confront the reality of spiritual wickedness as an individual, a father, a ministry practitioner, and a theologian. In order to survive with my sanity intact, I have studied spiritual warfare. What I have learned has allowed me to fight the good fight against the dark forces that have beat against me and those around me. It is from this perspective that I write this book.

The first three chapters present selected episodes from my personal narrative. Remaining chapters describe aspects of spiritual warfare and anointed ministry from biblical and practical perspectives. Spiritual warfare stories illustrate the material in those chapters. None of the illustrations qualify as "preacher stories." Each represents an unembellished, real to life account.

Besides personal experience, this book utilizes interview data and field research. For example, in 2015, I researched Latino Pentecostalism,

INTRODUCTION

folk religion, and spiritual warfare in Costa Rica and Colombia. In 2016, I studied spiritual warfare in Nigeria. Additionally, ministers from four continents have contributed personal anecdotes from their ministries. I have also included firsthand reports from my students. Most importantly, I am qualified to write this book because I am a warfare practitioner. During my spare time, I do inner healing, deliverance ministry, home cleansings, spiritual counseling, spiritual mapping, and all manner of power ministry as the Lord provides opportunity.

I must confess that personal experience looms large in this book. I hesitate to dwell too heavily on my circumstances because it boasts of hubris and shows a striking lack of detached perspective. Still, I don't know how to tell the story that I want to tell without including personal reflection. I justify this on two grounds.

First, personal experience helps one understand the biblical narrative. For example, when Paul declares that we fight against "the rulers, against the authorities, against the powers of this dark world and against the spiritual forces of evil in the heavenly realms" (Eph 6:12), he is speaking from personal experience. I have insight into his theology because I have shared in the same struggle. In short, the biblical narrative about spiritual warfare contains personal reflection.

Second, spiritual warfare isn't an academic subject that one can study from a distance. One must engage it to understand what the Scriptures teach about it. Mostly I smile when I read books written by academics and armchair theologians who pontificate on spiritual warfare themes from a safe distance. Immediately, I can tell which authors are practitioners and which are detached critics. For my part, I read the biblical material on spiritual warfare in light of my encounter with evil supernaturalism. They inform each other.

Finally, I would be remiss if I didn't acknowledge the great debt that I owe to Charles Kraft. Not only is he a pioneer in inner healing, he was a participant with John Wimber and C. Peter Wagner in the Third Wave "Signs and Wonders" Revival at Fuller Seminary in the late 1980s. His quiet teaching, personal reflections, and many books have enabled me to hold theory, theology, and practice together. I will forever cherish the classes that we have taught together.

*Section One*

What I Didn't Learn In Seminary

1

Antecedents

Shadows of a Looming Darkness

As a veteran of an unexpected adventure, Bilbo Baggins knew a thing or two about unforeseen journeys when he warned his settled nephew about inevitability. "It is a dangerous business, Frodo, going out of your door... You step into the Road, and if you don't keep your feet, there is no knowing where you might be swept off to. Do you realize that this is the very path that goes through Mirkwood, and that if you let it, it might take you to the Lonely Mountains or even further and to worse places?"[1]

Simply put, you can run from your destiny, but you can't escape it. Your fate will find you out. It is better to don your hiking shoes, take hold of your walking stick, and pursue the pending venture than to sit in your comfortable chair and fret about what lies ahead.

The ancient Chinese philosopher Laozi understood this truth when he asserted that a journey of a thousand miles begins with a single step. If you fixate on the enormity of the quest that lies before you, you will never leave your home. In truth, one can't complete an adventure that one doesn't begin. Consider Odysseus. If the epic hero had known that he wouldn't return to his home or see his beloved Penelope for twenty years when he set sail from Ithaca to fight in the Trojan War, he might have stayed put. Because he accepted the challenge and chased after his destiny, the entire world still recounts his exploits.

---

1. Tolkien, *The Fellowship of the Ring, Being the first Part of the Lord of the Rings*, 72.

Section One: What I Didn't Learn In Seminary

Often, I have contemplated my inertia when conjuring the motivation to complete a long jog. For me, Laozi's observation is self-evident. Once I take the first step, I will always finish my run. In fact, except for the time I fell and broke my leg, I have never failed to finish a run that I began. As such, the philosopher was correct when he avowed that taking the first step is the secret to completing a long journey.

Yet, in my case, taking the first step is only half the battle because a host of hindering or enabling antecedents determines whether I will stop what I'm doing and start my run. Often, inclement weather, work obligations, or family needs have sidetracked my good intentions. At other times, a pending physical fitness test, the need for stress release, or sheer desire have overpowered my resistance and driven me to run. As such, a long jog is connected to and influenced by preceding events that decide if I will or will not take the first step. Getting back to Laozi, the real secret to completing a long journey is overcoming the inertia that keeps one from taking the first step.

When I was a young adult, many inhibitors deterred me from taking the first step into spiritual warfare. I believed in demons because the Bible said that they existed; however, this intellectual assent didn't affect how I lived my life. Truthfully, I didn't face demons or fight against them because an inner Pollyanna convinced me that they wouldn't bother me if I ignored them. Ultimately, an accumulation of demonic encounters overwhelmed my internal inertia and pushed me to start my journey. In the language of Thomas Kuhn, I went through a "paradigm shift."[2]

Before I began my quest, I avoided deliverance ministry. I had seen the crazy excesses of televangelists, endured sensational Hollywood docudramas, and talked to Christians who saw demons under every rock. From my vantage point, those who practiced deliverance ministry seemed emotionally unbalanced and theologically compromised. Even though I wondered about the growing number of deliverance tabernacles and set-the-captives-free outreach centers that dotted the landscape of my city, I didn't want to be bothered by demons or those who cast them out. I never imagined that God, the Fates, or bad karma had destined me to become one of "those" people.

---

2. A paradigm shift is a fundamental change in approach or underlying assumptions. Often, it is associated with new insights and scientific breakthroughs. For more information on paradigm shifts, see Cohen, *Paradigm Shift*.

Antecedents

A Haunted Barracks in Okinawa

While serving as a battalion chaplain with the Fleet Marine Force in Okinawa (1990–1993), the Marines in one of my barracks complained about bizarre spiritual disturbances. The paranormal activities adversely affected their sleep and their ability to concentrate at work. After the Company Commander flippantly mentioned the situation at a staff meeting, the Battalion Commander told me to check things out. The next day, I toured the affected barracks and talked with the junior Marines who lived in them. When I examined the duty log, I saw cryptic references to an assortment of strange happenings.

At first, the reticent warriors didn't want to discuss the problem. However, after a respected corporal came forward, others began to talk. Over the next few hours, I spoke to several small groups of animated Marines. Everyone recounted the same phantasmagorical story with slightly different specifics. The following day, I received a stack of handwritten statements that described the problem and chronicled what had transpired. For many years, I kept the statements in a file and reviewed them from time to time to remember my introduction to spiritual warfare.

In short, evil spirits had infested the barracks. Many reported seeing apparitions. Eight had physical wounds including scratch marks and bruising. One showed me a ripped shirt and what appeared to be claw marks on his back. He maintained that an evil being had descended from the ceiling and injured him. Another had wounds on his arm. Several described the evil entity in lurid details. The existence of physical evidence and the consistency of the stories ruled out mass hysteria. Plus, these warriors were trained to render battlefield assessments while remaining calm under fire. Boot camp and infantry training school had prepared these Marines to combat human aggressors to include nuclear, biological, and chemical agents. However, they weren't trained to fight supernatural enemies. In the face of a dark and menacing aggressor that descended through the ceilings and attacked at will, they were as vulnerable as shipwrecked sailors trying to stay afloat in shark-infested seas.

In a vain attempt to ward off the specters, the Marines armed themselves with a variety of natural armaments. A small retractable shovel called an entrenching tool became the weapon of choice. The e-tool is standard issue with their 782 gear. Mostly, they use it in the field when they go to the bathroom, dig foxholes, and fill sandbags. In a pinch, it can be used for personal protection. Many of the bewildered Marines slept with their e-tools by their sides. When disturbed, they swatted at the spiritual interlopers like a person whacks at a pesky fly with a flyswatter. Others attempted folk remedies that included good luck charms and praying blessings over themselves. One endeavored to empower his e-tool with a special incantation that he learned while playing Dungeons and Dragons. Another requested a container of holy water so he could apply it to the corners of his room.

When I shared my findings with the Company Commander and the First Sergeant, they expressed curiosity and mild amusement but remained uncharacteristically detached. Because anxious, tired, and distracted Marines aren't mission-ready Marines, the command wanted a solution. Furthermore, the Battalion CO expected me to be an expert on all things related to religion including the paranormal. In truth, it didn't matter what I or anyone else believed about the haunting, the problem needed to be fixed.

During further investigation, a Marine confided that many had seen one of the evil beings while conducting a seance. Supposedly, they wanted to contact the demon to discover why it harassed them. Also, many played Dungeons and Dragons in their free time. Some participants began to identify with the characters that they played. Additionally, contractors had built their barracks on a ridge that featured a bloody assault in World War II. Battlegrounds and massacre sites have been linked to increased paranormal activity.[3]

After considering all the options, I hypothesized that occult activity by individuals in the barracks had given whatever was tormenting the Marines access to the berthing area. The afflicted Marines concurred with my assessment. Since everyone wanted to fix the problem, we performed a blessing on the barracks and asked the Marines not to do anything that "invited" the specters to return. Everyone agreed to restrict occult activities. Also, we moved Dungeons and Dragons play to a detached area. Peace returned to the barracks, the Marines slept, and the command was happy.

The Strange Case of the Man in a Fetal Position

On a quiet Saturday evening in July 1999, as I completed the final touches of my Sunday sermon, a desperate person called and requested a pastoral visit. Because I didn't know him, I intended to put him off until Monday.

---

3. In *The Twilight Labyrinth*, George Otis offers many examples to explain why evil lingers where it does. Also, a Google search of "ghosts on battlefields" will return many pages of reports that substantiate this claim.

However, a quiet pleading in his voice convinced me that I needed to attend to his needs.

Several times I turned in the wrong direction on unmarked dirt roads while searching for the man's address. When I finally arrived at his ranch-style house in the middle of nowhere, a short hunched over middle-aged man greeted me at the door. Upon entering his home, I noticed that he had decorated a ledge that encircled his living room with empty whiskey bottles. Quickly, I became aware of several other facts. He dispatched trucks from his house; he rarely left his residence; a large kyphosis hump on the top of his spine marred his self-image; his girlfriend had recently broken up with him; and, he had an alcohol problem. To top it off, I sensed that he might be suicidal.

When we spoke, pain mingled with desperation animated his conversation. His sad story made my heart ache. At some point, I told him about Jesus. He seemed quite receptive. After explaining the plan of salvation, I asked him if he wanted to receive Jesus as his Lord and Savior. Eagerly, he responded in the positive. However, when I closed my eyes and began to pray for him, my spine tingled, and cold perspiration dampened my forehead. In my spirit, I sensed that a thick, suffocating darkness had descended on the room. When I finally opened my eyes, I saw the man curled up in a fetal position close to my feet. Wild animal sounds reverberated. Bubbling saliva freely oozed from his mouth and pooled around his grimaced face. His glassy eyes stared in a blank and tormented gaze.

During many years of full-time ministry, I had never encountered anything like this. In my heart, I knew that this day would come. Still, I was wholly unprepared for the demonic confrontation when it happened. Indeed, none of my seminary professors or ministry mentors had told me how to handle this type of ministry encounter.

As I watched the man, I remembered the story about the Gadarene demoniac that fled from the tombs to meet Jesus when he got out of his boat (Matt 8:28–34). Jesus didn't run from the demons that haunted the poor man. Instead, he confronted them. At that moment, I prayed for help. Not knowing what to do, I simply followed my instincts. Mustering up my courage, I began to bind the demons as I spoke the name of Jesus over the man. Soon the man emerged from his stupor. Tears dripped from his eyes. He sounded confused and ashamed.

Since I didn't know how to complete the intervention, I asked the man to meet me in the prayer chapel after the eleven o'clock service the next day.

Section One: What I Didn't Learn In Seminary

Unfortunately, in the bustle of Sunday morning, I forgot about the conversation. Because I conducted three successive Sunday morning services, assistant pastors ministered in the prayer chapel after each service. They offered communion, anointed with oil, prayed with people, and provided pastoral care. While I was greeting my parishioners after the eleven o'clock service, an alarmed person pulled me aside and told me that they had an emergency in the prayer chapel. I instantly remembered my promise and loudly squawked, "Oh no!"

By the time I arrived, the man had fallen into another demonic stupor. The agitated demons were putting on quite a show. The assistant pastor working in the prayer chapel looked at me in bewilderment. I told her to take the people out of the chapel. Then I went through my newly learned ritual of binding the spirits as I asked God to release him from their control. After the demons had subsided, I sent the man home with the promise that I would get back to him.

As the man drove off, I crossed the street to our Hispanic chapel. A deeply spiritual man by the name of Reyes Martinez gave leadership to our Hispanic congregation. When I told him about my problem, he knew what to do. The next morning, the Hispanic pastor, an assistant pastor, a retired Lutheran minister, and I met to discuss our plans. The Lutheran minister and our Hispanic pastor conferred about procedural details. They explained how they would proceed and told me what to expect. They assured me that everything would be ok. In case the man vomited during the exorcism, they procured an empty bucket and a lot of towels.

After the meeting, I called the man and asked him if he would meet with me at my office. When he arrived, I told him that we wanted to free him from his demons by performing an exorcism. Without hesitation, he consented to the proposed intervention. Next, the Lutheran minister interviewed the man. He asked a lot of questions that revealed points of entrance and spiritual strongholds. The assistant pastor took notes. The Hispanic pastor and I provided a prayer covering. When the Lutheran pastor completed the interview, he led the man to renounce his sins, forgive those who had hurt him, and accept the forgiveness of Jesus. As the man prayed to receive Jesus, the demons tried to intervene. However, the minister shut them down.

At this point, the Lutheran minister began to pull the demons out. Nothing spectacular occurred. In fact, it was a bit anticlimactic. When the pastor called the demons by name, he spoke with authority. He controlled the entire process. The exorcism was as precise and straightforward as a medical procedure. As the demons left, the man would cough and gag, but he didn't vomit. The man was delivered in less than thirty minutes.

The aftermath was dramatic. In the coming months, God freed the man from his encumbrances. His former girlfriend was so impressed with his progress that she reconnected with him. He became a mainstay at every church function. Most importantly, joy characterized his new life.

Not everyone shared his delight. In the immediate aftermath of his deliverance, the man visited his home United Methodist Church in Eastern Pennsylvania. When he shared his story with the congregation, the pastor became so irate that she called me on the phone. In her words, I had engaged in spiritual abuse, clergy malpractice, and unethical behavior. She threatened to report the incident to my bishop and file ecclesiastical charges against me. In closing, she reminded me that demons are not real and that seminary educates professional clergy to demythologize the text. In her words, United Methodism is much too sophisticated to believe that Jesus dealt with real demons.

I didn't help my cause when I burst out with uproarious laughter. The minister's ignorance mixed with arrogance blinded her to the spiritual world. I wondered if she would have held to her anti-supernatural philosophy if she had been with me when the man's demons manifested.

A Woman Suffering from Post-Abortion Stress Syndrome

Two weeks after the episode with the demonized man, I had another encounter with evil supernaturalism. A woman in the church I pastored suffered from post-abortion stress syndrome. Every year at the anniversary of her abortion, she had a demonic episode that led to a suicide attempt. Each year, the suicide attempts became more potent. In the interim, she had mini-attacks. Most were punctuated by rage and detached thinking.

The woman grew up in a Christian home. Often, she had vowed that she would never have an abortion. While away at college, a man who offered to take her home from a party sexually assaulted her. Later, she came to understand that he had raped her. To complicate the matter, she became pregnant. She wasn't ready to deal with the rape and was totally unprepared to have a baby. She did the only thing that made sense to her at that moment. She terminated the pregnancy.

Section One: What I Didn't Learn In Seminary

In the immediate aftermath, grief and shame flooded over her. Not only did she lose her virginity to a man who didn't love her, she believed that she compromised her salvation by having an abortion. She had dreamed of being used by God to do ministry. In her mind, God couldn't use a woman who had an abortion. She also felt that God didn't love her anymore. After all, how could God love a woman who broke a vow and killed a baby?

Soon after her abortion, she found herself on a bridge contemplating suicide. Her life passed before her as she considered her next step. As she summoned the courage to kill herself, God spoke to her in an audible voice. He said, "The thing that you are planning to do will prevent me from fulfilling my plans with you." Just then, she melted before God and felt a deep peace. The grace of God flowed over her. She realized that God still loved her and that he still had plans for her life.

In the aftermath, she got professional counseling and volunteered for a pro-life ministry team on her college campus. Often, she shared her story with desperate young women who were seeking an abortion. Unfortunately, she continued to suffer from frequent demonic attacks without realizing that the demons were tormenting her. In some warped way, she believed that she deserved her suffering.

All the attacks followed a similar pattern. Something would trigger an emotional auto-response. Often it had to do with a feeling of rejection, unworthiness, or being out of control. When something piqued the emotional wound, it released uncontrollable anger. In time, the anger would morph into a rage. During a typical attack, cursing and hostility poisoned the air. After the spiritual assault started, it couldn't be curtailed until it ran its course. The cycle ended with feelings of worthlessness, helplessness, and suicidal ideation. Sometimes it included physical violence.

The day in question was an anniversary attack. As we had discussed, the husband called me when the demonic episode began. When I saw the woman, she was beside herself with anger and rage. Soon, vulgarity confronted me. Not wanting to escalate the situation, I began to whisper a praise chorus from the Gaither Vocal Band, "Jesus, Jesus, Jesus, There's Just Something about that Name." When I reached the second stanza, the woman screeched, "Stop saying that name!" Then she picked me up by my collar and pounded me against the kitchen wall. Afterward, she ran off to her bedroom and locked the door behind her. Her supernatural strength should have scared me. However, it just made me more determined. Since I knew where this was heading, I resolved to confront the demons.

Antecedents

The husband used an Allen wrench to open the door. When he did, we found the woman crying on the side of her bed. A loaded rifle sat on her lap. Before we had entered the room, she had placed the barrel in her mouth and tried to end it all. Technical difficulties saved her. Under normal circumstances, I would counsel pastors to dial 911 and not to confront a suicidal person who held a loaded rifle. However, my heart told me to go forward.

I sat beside her and began to comfort her. She sobbed lightly. She didn't make eye contact. I suggested that she didn't want to commit suicide. She agreed. However, she added that she wanted the pain to stop. She couldn't live with the torment any longer. I asked her if she would allow me to cast out the demons that were tormenting her. She consented. Since I had already counseled with her and her husband about the issue, I already knew her story and didn't need to do an interview. Rather, I let the Holy Spirit lead me. Over the next twenty minutes, I cast out many vile demons. They left with loud burps. The spirit of death was the hardest to dislodge. Eventually, it also left. When we finished, she continued to burp for an hour or so.

Being set free from the tormenting demons signaled the start of her healing process. However, the woman had to make peace with her past and mend her wounded soul before she could walk in freedom because the demons had been attached to her damaged emotions. Thankfully, a female counselor from a local Pentecostal church did counseling with her. With God's help and the patient support of her family, she seized the opportunity and claimed her victory.

Obviously, I was very excited. I had completed a solo exorcism and the demons had obeyed me. Most importantly, the woman found new life. Following this event, I became acutely aware of spiritual warfare. Still, I did not look for demons under every rock or seek more opportunities to practice deliverance ministry. Instead, I adopted a wait and see policy. Consequently, I did not do any other exorcisms for many years.

2

Engaging the Battle

AFTER COMPLETING A TOUR with Navy Europe, my family and I moved from London to Ashland, Ohio in 2002. In addition to starting my new job as a professor at the seminary, my wife and I bought our first house. Our new residence rested on a bucolic knoll that adjoined the city cemetery. Unbeknownst to us, the dwelling had an intriguing history.

A previous owner moved out very suddenly due to an acute problem with his wife. Rumor says that she died from an accidental drowning. The next owners left their teenage sons alone in the home for many months when they moved to Michigan. We found stark evidence of their sexual exploits. For example, we discovered a large stash of twenty or more trophy panties of all sorts hidden in a compartment in the ceiling by their downstairs bedroom. In addition to underage drinking and hardcore partying, it is possible that they sexually assaulted young women. We also have reason to believe that the teenagers engaged in occult activity. All such behavior invites spiritual bondage and gives demonic entities an open invitation to harass those who occupy the dwelling.

My House Is Haunted

Six months after moving in, we experienced our first demonic attack. When the attack began, I was viewing an ethnographic video on exorcism for a cultural anthropology class that I was teaching. Since exorcism is common in most traditional societies, I previewed exorcism videos from Islam, African tribal religions, Latin American shamans, and the like. At the time of

Engaging the Battle

the attack, I was watching a Roman Catholic priest perform a dramatic rite of exorcism. In the video, the demons shrieked as the priest read the liturgy and brandished a raised crucifix in the face of a cowering man. When the priest flicked holy water on the man, the demons shouted that the drops burned like fire. If anything could have provoked the ire of angry demons, that movie would have done it.

While watching the video, loud knocking sounds began to reverberate throughout the house. I didn't know that the sounds came from agitated demons. Instead, I wrongly believed that my older children were pounding on the wall. Since my wife worked the night shift at the local hospital, I feared that the noise would wake up the baby and I would have to stop my work. With indignation, I marched downstairs to the family area where I found the kids huddled in front of the computer. When I confronted them about the ruckus, they denied making it. They retorted that I was making the noise.

With curious interest, my fifteen-year-old son and I walked upstairs to find the source of the pounding. As we ascended the stairs, the knocking stopped. At the same time, the latch on the door that we were about to open began to go up and down rapidly. It made a loud chattering sound as the lever moved precipitously without any human assistance. My son turned red and ran. I didn't touch the latch. Rather, I stood in stark terror as I stared at it. In disbelief, I muttered, "This isn't supposed to happen." Out of desperation and fear for my family, I began to rebuke the invisible power. My prayers became more animated as I felt the Holy Spirit rising in me. Eventually, it stopped. Afterward, I walked through the house and prayed over each room. No one slept well that night.

Over the next weeks, the computer typed by itself on a regular basis. While playing Ping-Pong in the family room, we would watch the words fly across the computer screen. Ironically, the typing didn't spell anything that we could understand. It is possible that the typist was communicating in a different language. It is also possible that it typed nonsense words simply because it wanted to harass us.

After a while, we tried to ignore the disturbances. At times, the demons made it hard to ignore them. For example, one day my son and I were playing with our last orange Ping-Pong ball. After a hard hit, we watched the ball go behind some books in an enclosed bookcase behind me. We heard it rattling between the wooden bookcase and the books. Since it was an enclosed shelf, reason told us that the ball had to be where it landed.

Section One: What I Didn't Learn In Seminary

However, we couldn't find it. In desperation, we removed all the books from the shelf and the adjoining shelves. In vain, we searched for fifteen minutes. Finally, we realized that the ball was taken and that we couldn't finish playing Ping-Pong. A week later, after we bought white Ping-Pong balls, the orange one reappeared in plain sight on top of a book at the exact place where we last saw it. When I observed it resting on top of the book, I said, "Oh, there it is. Silly me. How did I miss that?"

As recently as last month, my daughter hit a ball that went into an enclosed corner between two bookshelves. The cat chased the errant ball to the corner and then jumped back as if something startled her. Afterward, she stood at a distance and peered into the corner. When my daughter went to get the ball, it had vanished. Of course, it had no place to go. By the laws of reason, it had to be in the enclosed area. My daughter and I are still waiting for it to return.

The disappear-and-reappear trick became a favorite game. One day while I was coming home from class, my thumb drive vanished from my pocket. After mounting an enormous search for it, I finally had to recreate the lost files. Three weeks later, the thumb drive reappeared in the same pocket from which it disappeared even though the pants had been worn and washed three times since the thumb drive first dematerialized. I should add, it appeared while I was wearing the pants. I knew that it returned when it materialized in my pocket. Strangely, it still worked. Since a thumb drive can't survive washing and drying, I wonder where it went when it vanished from my pocket.

Keys were a preferred target. One day while going out to my car, I set my keys down on a lampstand, so I could retrieve something from my bedroom. When I returned thirty seconds later, the keys had disappeared. I was the only person in the house. The next day, they reappeared on the lampstand in the exact place I had left them the previous day. Of course, the search for the spare key caused me to be late for class. That is part of the harassment game.

Another time I placed my keys in the car cup holder when I dropped my child off at the daycare center. I always put my keys in the cup holder when I carried my daughter into the building. This time, when I returned to the car, they were missing. After searching for ten minutes, I walked to class. Later, a student and I carefully examined the car together. She had to drive me home to retrieve my spare key. Three weeks later, the lost keys reappeared in the cup holder as if they had never disappeared. Somehow, I always knew when the taken objects were returned. It was as if I had a surge of faith and was aware of what would happen before it happened.

A third time my car keys vanished when I came home from work and set them down on an outside bench. Literally, I bent over and pulled two dandelions. As soon as I straightened up, the keys were gone. I knew where I had laid the keys but couldn't convince others of this. So, I went through the formality of looking for my lost keys with my family. Since my spare key for this car lacked a factory installed chip, the car's anti-theft system kept it from working. Consequently, I couldn't use my car and had no other means of transportation.

For a week, I bummed rides or walked everywhere as I patiently waited for my lost keys to return. Finally, my wife made me buy a new key. To do so, I had to get my car towed to the dealer and pay $250 to program the new key. You can guess what happened when I came home. The missing keys were on the bench where I had left them the previous week. When I got out of the car, I picked up the lost keyring and walked into the house with the new key in one hand and the old key in the other.

Ping Pong balls and keys weren't the only things that went missing. After returning from a short trip, I discovered that my shaving kit was missing from my suitcase. It contained expensive medicine, an electric razor, and a dental apparatus that cost $500. Even though I remembered packing the shaving kit in my suitcase before we left, my wife made me call the hotel where we stayed. The staff couldn't find it. My wife and I scoured the car and the suitcase many times. Losing valuable stuff provokes frustration, squanders precious time, and causes you to incur unplanned expenses.

When we gave up the search, I put the empty and unzipped suitcase by the stairs with the intention of placing it in a downstairs closet. With intense frustration, I replaced the medications and paid for a new dental device. A few weeks later, I picked up the empty suitcase. Amazingly, as I lifted it from the floor, the missing shaving kit fell out of it and landed in front of me as if it had always been in the suitcase. Nothing was missing from it.

Just last month, my wife left an unused roll of stamps on a stack of unsent Christmas cards. When she went to put the stamps on the envelopes, the roll was missing. She and I removed everything from the stand on which the envelopes and roll of stamps had rested. We also checked the floor around the area. Finally, my wife returned to the post office and bought a new roll of stamps. When we came into the kitchen after buying the new stamps, the missing roll of stamps was resting on the stack of envelopes as if it had never gone missing.

If I tried to list all the things that disappeared and reappeared, I would fill up an entire chapter. Interestingly, even though Americans seem incredulous when I talk to them about the problem of missing things, Africans, Native Americans, and Hispanics understand it well. Traditional societies often blame the problem on trickster spirits. Because this is such a common problem, Roman Catholicism has a saint to help people find lost things.[1]

Stealing objects wasn't the worst problem. Sometimes the demons moved items or materialized things in unexpected places. For example, one night I pushed the nursery door open to check on my toddler. When I tried to pull it closed, something relocated a toy zebra from the toybox to the pathway of the door as I tried to close it. The toy zebra was standing on its four legs. It could not have been there before I attempted to shut the door because the force of opening the door would have pushed it out of the way.

Additionally, the sound of creaking footsteps on our wooden floors frightened our babysitters so badly that none would come back. One night when I returned from class, even my wife was afraid to go back to the nursery because she imagined that an invisible "thing" was walking on the wooden floors. As one might expect, I marched to the nursery and refused to surrender my little girl to the harassment.

One of the most unusual moments occurred during family devotions. While reading John Wesley's correspondence about the poltergeist at the Wesley Rectory in Epworth,[2] we heard a loud bang. We thought that the cat had fallen through the ceiling. Upon investigation, the cat was with us. However, all the books from the top shelf of my bookcase had been thrown to the ground. The bookcase was still standing erect and the shelves were undisturbed. Even though most of the books were haphazardly scattered on the floor, something had neatly stacked the spiritual warfare books directly in front of the bookshelf. When my wife saw the neatly stacked pile of spiritual warfare books, she gazed in disbelief. Finally, she suggested that the books were stacked because they must have fallen on top of each other. Since the top shelf was over six feet high, I divined a different meaning.

---

1. See St. Anthony Di Padua Da Montefalcione Society, Inc., "Who Is Saint Anthony?"
2. See Wesley, *The Haunting of Epworth Rectory*.

Closing the Loop on Missing Things

Between 2003 and 2014 I had many adventures in spiritual warfare including direct confrontations with evil supernaturalism in many forms. During these years, I also learned more about spiritual warfare and how to flow with the Spirit when doing anointed ministry. Later, I will recount a series of encounters that occurred in 2014. Before I do, I need to give some closure to my problem with disappearing items.

After 2003, disappearing and reappearing items vexed my life. Keys, wallets, cell phones, checkbooks, and important books routinely went missing. One night a critical file disappeared from my computer while I was using it. Eventually, a Microsoft technician logged remotely into my computer. He promised me that he could find it. My computer automatically saves files to the cloud and my hard drive. Plus, it has temporary "AutoSaved" files. Finally, the technician said that the file didn't exist and that it never existed. After I had reworked the material, the lost file reappeared on my computer. Because of this event, I now save everything on a removable flash drive and I send myself an electronic copy via email.

In 2013, while complaining to God about this problem over which I felt completely helpless, he taught me how to stop the demons from taking valuable things from me. As I meditated, God told me to "Bind them to you" (Matt 16:9 and 18:18). At first, I thought about the ecclesiastical debates that surround binding and loosing as they pertain to the authority of Peter. People who do deliverance ministry also refer to these texts when they "bind" demons. When talking about binding demons, they also reference Matthew 12:29. The text says, "How can anyone enter a strong man's house and carry off his possessions unless he first ties up [binds] the strong man? Then he can plunder his house." In the context of Matthew 16 and 18, binding and loosing relate to the keys of the kingdom and the ability to exercise divine authority. In some way, God has given the church the authority to bind and loose in the spiritual realm. That authority extends to demons but isn't limited to them. It flows from the Christian's positional authority in Christ.

As I meditated more carefully on the word that I received from God, I realized that God wanted me to bind my things to me. This unorthodox thought didn't align with any traditional interpretation of the Scriptures. However, desperation drove me to experiment. Afterward, I prayed this simple prayer over all my important things. "I bind this item to me in the name of Jesus Christ, and I proclaim that it pertains to me. It may not be taken from me." Since binding these things to me, none has been taken from me. Other things have been taken, but not the ones over which I prayed. Now when I am annoyed because something is taken, I remind myself that I should have bound the item to me.

I need to add a disclaimer. All humans misplace things from time to time. That also happens to me. However, losing a thing is very different from having it taken from you. When I misplace something, I can readily find it when I think carefully, retrace my steps, and see things that are in front of me. I can also practice being mindful when I lay something down. However, no matter how well you search, you cannot find a thing that the demons have taken from you until it is returned.

Allow me to offer a very fresh update on this. Many years ago, my checkbook mysteriously disappeared from my desk. We did many exhausting searches for it. Finally, I canceled all the checks for a $25 fee. While typing this section, I looked up from my computer and saw my missing checkbook on the shelf in front of me. It just reappeared on my desk in the same place where I left it many years ago. I don't know how it disappeared or why it reappeared now. Since the checkbook reappeared, I called my bank and discovered that I could use the checks since they only block a check for two years. That is a good thing because I forgot to reorder checks and I needed to use them!

As everything that disappears eventually reappears in the very place where it was taken, I must assume that a spiritual rule stipulates the return of stolen items. I don't know what the rule is, but I can postulate that there is one because of the regularity associated with it. Like the physical realm, the spiritual realm is governed by rules. God designed creation so that rules dictate how things operate. In these days, spiritual warfare practitioners have learned many of the laws associated with the spirit realm.[3] With time, inspiration, and experimentation, practitioners will learn more about the laws that govern the spiritual realm. As they do, they will become better equipped to wage spiritual warfare with more precision and more success.

---

3. Charles Kraft has identified many of the rules that govern our interaction with the spiritual realm in his groundbreaking book, *The Rules of Engagement*. C. Peter Wagner, Derek Prince, and Cindy Primes have also published books on this theme. Kraft re-examines this material in *Power Encounter in Spiritual Warfare*.

3

Dark Tide Rising

THE SPIRITUALLY ATTUNED FLOW with the daily rhythm of spiritual warfare. I've seen this in my life and in the lives of others. More specifically, when the kingdom mantle settles upon a believer, that person will approach everyday Christianity in a way that reflects the New Testament example. Intercessory prayer, casting out demons, praying for the sick, getting words of knowledge, and giving spiritual counsel become routine. However, there are times when the intensity of spiritual warfare significantly increases.

As was alluded to in the Forward, the early spring of 2014 witnessed a sharp uptick in spiritual warfare in Ashland. It started when spirits physically restrained a student while attending a class. When she fled the class, two other students followed. The spirits also attacked them. They described being held down against their will. This event caused them to become super agitated.

In the aftermath, the professor of that class, the students, and I prayed over the room in which the second attack occurred. The area in question displays cultural artifacts including Canaanite fertility idols. An ancient fresco of Hercules fighting the Hydra drew the group's attention. All felt intense heat coming from it as we extended our hands toward the painting while in prayer. We assumed that the picture had been dedicated to Hercules because it animated spiritual power. According to Greek mythology, the son of Zeus was born a demigod but was given divine status as a god. A cult of devotees worshiped him in the ancient world. Whoever created the ancient fresco would have been aware of this. Most likely, the fresco was commissioned for religious reasons.

SECTION ONE: WHAT I DIDN'T LEARN IN SEMINARY

Breaking Demonic Associations

The group travailed in prayer until it severed any connections between the artifacts and any demons with which they might have been associated. Once an object is dedicated to a god, an evil spirit can maintain a connection to the object until the linkage is broken by invoking the name of Jesus over it or by destroying it. When dedicated items are relocated, the demons associated with them may gain access to the new place. Spiritual warfare literature affirms this.[1]

Charles Kraft argues that material objects can be empowered when they are dedicated to God (e.g., sacraments or holy water) or to the Evil One (e.g., idols or amulets). According to Kraft, many missionaries have endured needless harassment because they didn't understand this principle when they brought demonically empowered souvenirs into their homes.[2] In the case of the Hercules fresco and Canaanite idols, we claimed these artifacts for the true God and blessed them in his name; thus, breaking the old linkage and establishing a new one.

The New Testament church struggled with the issue of empowered items. For example, the Jerusalem Council told Gentile Christians to abstain from things polluted by idols (Acts 15:20 and 21:25). The prohibition meant that they couldn't eat food sacrificed to false gods. Revelation 2:14 re-emphasizes the injunction against eating food sacrificed to idols and threatens a judgment against those who violate the rule. First Corinthians 10:18–22 uncovers the reason for the food ban. "The sacrifices of pagans are offered to demons, not to God, and I do not want you to be participants with demons. You cannot drink the cup of the Lord and the cup of demons too; you cannot have a part in both the Lord's Table and the table of demons. Are we trying to arouse the Lord's jealousy? Are we stronger than he?" (I Cor 10:20–22).[3] Even though an idol is nothing, food sacrificed to

---

1. John Hagee offers many convincing examples of objects that convey demonic powers in *The Three Heavens*, 127–131. The story about Kachina Dolls is riveting. In the Introduction to *Handbook for Spiritual Warfare*, Ed Murphy tells how his daughter was badly demonized after she wore a gifted necklace that was an empowered pentagram.

2. Charles Kraft discusses this issue in many publications under the topic of form and meaning. I recommend *The Evangelical's Guide to Spiritual Warfare*, 94–101. For an academic perspective, read the debate between Charles Kraft and Robert Priest in Rommen, *Spiritual Power and Missions*, 96–100.

3. First Corinthians 8 seems to go in a different direction with the prohibition against eating food sacrificed to idols. In this chapter, Paul warns believers who eat food sacrificed to idols not to use their liberty to cause harm to the weaker brothers. That is, if a

idols may not be eaten because it is offered to demons. For that reason, a believer will suffer harmful spiritual consequences if he eats food dedicated to idols (demons).

Based on Paul's teaching, some see a parallel between the New Testament proscription against eating food sacrificed to idols and eating blessed communion elements. In the parallel, the dedicated communion elements convey a divine grace to the one who ingests them. In practice, the communion elements become holy when a clergyperson devotes them to God by means of a prayer of consecration. Afterward, the dedicated elements convey God's blessing to the person who consumes them because there is a real link between the blessed elements and God's real presence. In the end, the sacrament is efficacious because it transmits God's spiritual power (grace) and is a means by which God gains access to the believer.

Others argue that communion doesn't convey real grace to the believer. Instead, they insist that New Testament communion is an ordinance that commemorates Jesus' suffering on the cross. Of course, New Testament communion can be an ordinance and a sacrament at the same time. Regardless, many modern theologians shy away from the sacramental approach because they struggle with the worldview of the New Testament world. Plainly, the ancient Greek believer saw a theological connection between food dedicated to idols and food dedicated to God through communion. A firmer understanding of that relationship would revitalize how many modern Christians approach communion.

The Jerusalem Council's injunction against eating meat dedicated to idols caused problems for poor Gentile believers because food vendors sold dedicated meat at discounted prices. In fact, meat sacrificed to idols was a common source of nutrition. Thankfully, Paul offered Greek believers a practical workaround. They could nullify the demonic association by blessing the meat in Jesus' name. That is, in the same way that my friends and I blessed and rededicated the Canaanite idols to God, the Greek believers could bless and rededicate the meat that had been contaminated by idols to Jesus before they ate it.

In the end, Paul nuances the teaching of the Jerusalem Council. Instead of enforcing a strict prohibition, he advises the believers not to ask where the meat came from when they are invited to eat with an unbeliever.

Christian believes that one cannot eat food sacrificed to an idol without being contaminated by it, the believer of strong faith must not cause the person of weak faith to sin by encouraging him to eat food sacrificed to idols.

Rather, they are to invoke the name of Jesus over the food and eat it with thanksgiving. The demonically contaminated food will be sanctified (made holy and set apart to God) through the prayer. "For everything God created is good, and nothing is to be rejected if it is received with thanksgiving, because it is consecrated by the word of God and prayer" (1 Tm 4:4–5). For ancient Christians who lived in close proximity with pagan society, praying over food was not a ritualized "blessing of the bread" as in Judaism. In that world, it became a necessary way to push away the demonic influences that existed in the marketplace of life.

Back to the story, after the women who had been physically restrained came forward, others began to share stories about spiritual harassment and encounters with spiritual evil. One international student confided that a spirit awakened her at night by pulling on her leg. It didn't release her until she pleaded the blood of Jesus and cried out to God. A male student woke in the middle of the night with a jackal-headed figure standing over him. The being looked like Anubis from ancient Egypt. The god had a dog head and a human body. The being spoke to the student about lust.

While performing a dramatic deliverance for a student, an evil spirit told me that he gained access to the student's room through a picture on the wall. As I mentioned, dedicated artifacts and evil deeds can give evil spirits legal rights to specific spaces. That is why one must uncover past histories and attempt to undo whatever gave the demons access to a location. In this case, a charmed painting and the grievous sin of a former occupant served as the demon's link to the room.

Because spiritual harassment seemed like a routine occurrence, a group of female students banded together to pray for revival, to understand the spiritual topography, and to have mutual support. The group went by the name of the Amazons (female prayer warriors). A female faculty member facilitated the group. By invitation, I met with them on a regular basis.

A month after the first attack, my wife noticed that I had bruises on my chest. It looked like fingers had pressed on me. I attributed the black and blue marks to age. On the following Monday, I mentioned my bruising to the Amazons. To my shock, everyone in the group had marks on their bodies. For ten minutes, we showed each other our bruises. Some had severe black and blue marks. The faculty advisor also had bad bruising and some bleeding. One suggested that the marks were the stigmata. No one knew why they had bruising. They just appeared. As we tried to divine a meaning, we discerned a threat. We were vulnerable to attack. The powers wanted us to abandon our prevailing prayer. The threat made us more determined.

Problems with Sex Demons

Others disclosed that spirits were sexually molesting them. Before this, I had never encountered a person who confessed to having personal contact with an incubus spirit even though I knew about them through books, history, and movies. In a short timeframe, I came across five people who said that incubi harassed them. For example, while working with a badly demonized teenager, an incubus spirit manifested. I couldn't cast it out. Afterward, the nineteen-year-old told me that it had regular sex with her when she went to bed. According to her, it was better than any guy. It had a name and was like a friend. She didn't want to get rid of it. When I explained that it was a demon who abused her, she reluctantly consented to deliverance.

During the same period, a male student with whom I was doing inner healing confessed that he had sporadic encounters with a succubus spirit that he prayed for when he was a teenager. Like others, he enjoyed his encounters and wanted to hold on to it. A young Wiccan that I was evangelizing referred to his she-demon as his lover. He described it as a beautiful, sexy, romantic, caring, friend who gave him great advice. Even when I explained the dangers of this demon and urged the man to flee from it, he wouldn't let it go. He wanted his demon more than he desired freedom in Christ.

Are Sex Demons Real?

I believe that the phenomena associated with succubae and incubi spirits are real for many reasons. First, since 2014, others have described them to me. For example, recently, while working with a woman who suffered from dissociative identity disorder, I discovered an incubus demon who had entered her after she was raped at the tender age of twelve. The ensuing alter ego went by the name of Debbie. Soon after the rape, the sex spirit approached the girl by shaking the foot of her bed. Afterward, it had sex with her. Because the child had been groomed by prolonged molestation and had been dedicated to Satan by her family, she enjoyed the initial encounter with the sex demon. The attacks continued for thirty years. The dominant personality only had a vague memory of the first abuse. However, the alter ego had an excellent memory of it. Once I was able to connect with Debbie, we were able to cast out the incubus spirit.

Last year I had an epic battle with an incubus while trying to free a woman who desperately wanted freedom. A mental health counselor referred the client to me because she believed that the person was a victim of spirit rape. The client's story has parallels to the true-life story behind *The Entity* movie that was released in 1982.[4] Also, in *Ghost Sex, the Violation*, G. L. Davies carefully documents the phenomenon in the lives of many people over three generations.[5]

A few months ago, a friend from Ghana shared her struggle about a sex spirit. When she was a young child, she formed a soul-tie with an older girl. She desperately desired that the older girl would like her. When she became a teenager, she even worked a spare job so she could buy the older girl gifts in order to win her affection. However, despite her efforts, the older girl abused the relationship and emotionally harmed my friend. Over the years, my friend felt intense emotional pain because of the bad relationship but was unable to sever the soul-tie. When she became an adult, she immigrated to the United States. Afterward, a spirit in the guise of her friend started to have sex with my friend during her nightly dreams. When this happened, my friend would feel pain and have bodily fluids. Consequently, she has not been able to have a normal relationship with a man or enjoy sex since the attacks started.

Most recently, a desperate man called my office looking for help. When I interviewed him, he told me a sad tale. After his girlfriend left him, he tried to make her return to him by increasing his mind consciousness through transcendental meditation. He used crystals to help open his chakras. While increasing mind consciousness, a purported spirit guide offered to help him. Gladly, he allowed the spirit to have access to him. When he did, the spirit began to rape him on a daily basis. Besides humiliating him, it hurt his body. He turned to Christ because he wanted freedom.

---

4. Green, "The Entity: True Story About a Woman Who is Attacked by Invisible, Paranormal Forces."

5. Davies, *Ghost Sex: The Violation*. According to Davies, incubus sex is on the rise. He gives many convincing accounts that sound the same as the struggles of my clients who fight against incubi spirits. He offers three explanations. One, people are less religious today. Two, it is the result of sleep paralysis. Three, it is an alien abduction. I would add that cybersex, pornography, drugs, and sexual abuse also play a big part in deciding who will be victimized by it. As an aside, those who research alien abduction stories have reported that the use of Jesus' name stops the abductions. For an explanation of this phenomenon, see *Demonic Alien Abduction Stopped by Calling on Jesus Name*.

Second, history going back to 2500 BC documents the existence of sex spirits. In fact, every ancient civilization has stories about them. Even though the names of the sex spirits or gods change, the content remains similar. The stories don't appear to be the result of cultural diffusion. In ancient Mesopotamia, the father of Gilgamesh (the proto-Noah) is listed as Lilu, an incubus spirit. Greek mythology says that Zeus seduced the Princess Danae in the form of a golden shower. He took on the form of a satyr to seduce Antiope. People having sex with nymphs and gods is very common in Greek literature. In ancient Arabia, the sex spirit was called Qarinah. This spirit came from Egypt. In India, the incubus is called Mohini. In the Brazilian rainforests, it goes by the name Boto. People in southern Africa call it Tikoloshe. Hebrew folklore speaks about these spirits in the Kabbalah and Alphaber of Ben Sira. The most famous was called Lilith. Additionally, some have argued that Genesis 6:1–4 refers to incubi when it talks about the "sons of God" who had intercourse with the daughters of Adam and sired demigod children.

For obvious reasons, most people don't discuss their experiences with sex demons. Because of this, the phenomenon may be more extensive than people realize. In my opinion, if one conducted a confidential survey of the adult population in the world, eight to ten percent would affirm that they have encountered a sex spirit.

An Unfortunate Encounter with a Witch

During the time that I consulted with the Amazons, I had an inadvertent encounter with a witch. On the night in question, I carried C. Peter Wagner's book on territorial spirits into a local restaurant.[6] I felt called to do this and was ready to converse about it. Immediately, my server began to talk to me when she saw my book. After I explained the title and gave her a basic synopsis of the content, she stated that she was a lesbian, showed me some strange tattoos, and told me about the spirits that she channeled. Even though she channeled a lot of spirits, she said that she was attached to one spiritual helper who enabled her to have incredible power over other people. She re-engaged the conversation each time she returned to fill my empty coffee cup.

I listened and responded in a polite and interested manner to understand more about her and waited for an opportunity to tell her about Jesus.

6. Wagner, *Territorial Spirits*.

Evangelism never happened because she directed the conversation. Soon, I began to feel uncomfortable. The way she smiled at me when I paid the bill bothered me. By the time that I got to my car, my chest hurt and my head felt light. Immediately I recognized the signs. I see the same symptoms when I do deliverance with others. It means that their demons are aroused. In my case, it meant that I was undergoing a spiritual attack. When I finally reached my house, I prayed over myself and repelled the demons that were empowered against me. The self-cleansing was a profound and prolonged event that was accentuated by loud burping, an external sign that may accompany the casting out of demons.

I should add a note to prevent confusion. In previous ministry encounters, those who assisted me occasionally suffered from spiritual attacks even though we prayed a prayer of covering over ourselves before we began the ministry intervention. When they complained of physical pains and other symptoms, I took authority over them in the same way that I did the demonized person. Afterward, the symptoms went away. Perhaps the fleeing spirits attacked my helpers or the exorcism stirred up demons already present in the helpers. Both possibilities have value. Nevertheless, I hope that the demons which I cast out don't demonize my helpers or me; at least, I pray for that. I am willing to consider a third option—perhaps different demons attacked the helpers because we were casting out their colleagues.

From my perspective, I believe that a demonic attack on a Christian may have the obvious symptoms of demonization even if the person is not demonized. I speak about this reality in the chapter on soul-ties. When this happens, the person may respond positively to authority prayer. Since I have been on the receiving end of many demonic attacks even though I was walking close to the Lord and practicing regular self-deliverance, personal experience leads me to this conclusion.

Personal Attacks

During this season of increased spiritual warfare, the spiritual climate of my home changed. For a week, I tried to read Ed Murphy's, *The Spiritual Warfare Handbook* in preparation for an upcoming spiritual warfare class in June. However, every time I started to read I became fatigued and fell asleep within minutes. Literally, after a week of determined effort, I had only read the first chapter. Murphy wrote a profound book that helps people do effective spiritual warfare. Understandably, the enemy doesn't want people to read it.

When I finally realized that I was being attacked by a soporific (sleep) spirit, I rebuked the spirit and prayed over my reading area. Immediately, the sleep problem left me and I devoured the book without any problem. As an added benefit, I no longer fell asleep when I drove. Previously, I had often fallen asleep at the wheel. The problem began when I turned eighteen. On several occasions, I awoke after an unknown amount of time far down the road on which I was traveling. One time, I awoke in heavy traffic on the Pennsylvania Turnpike. All the cars were stopped. Fortunately, I was also stopped! I assume that God protected me.

I should add that sleep spirits are quite common. Recently, I met one when doing inner healing. The man reported that he couldn't concentrate, pray, or read his Bible. Every time that he tried to do so, he felt exhausted. When he came into my office, I felt exhausted. I began to yawn and had no emotional energy. While praying over him at the beginning of our session, I dozed off midway through my prayer. At that point, I recognized the problem and cleansed the area. Neither of us had any more sleep problems during that session.

The next time you are in church, look around and see if you can find evidence of a sleep spirit. They often manifest when there is anointed worship or a powerful sermon. Last year, I preached about the light shining in the darkness and the inability of Satan to overcome God's truth. The Holy Spirit was powerfully present. Incredibly, many people fell fast asleep as I was preaching. Afterward, one said that something came over her and she couldn't stay awake no matter how hard she tried. That is how the sleep demon keeps people dull to the word of God.

After working through my problems with Murphy's book, my family and I made a big mistake when we watched a Focus Features Film in which a Roman Centurion prayed to the god Mithras on several occasions.[7] Roman soldiers had a special relationship with this god. He migrated from Persia to Europe through Alexander the Great's soldiers. Persians called him Mithra. He is a powerful god that has many similarities to Jesus. The movie is an action adventure with a good plot. It teaches many good lessons and is fun to watch. Unfortunately, the prayers to Mithras opened some spiritual doors in our house. To be sure, we all felt conviction when the

---

7. The movie is called *The Eagle*, by Focus Features Films.

main character prayed to Mithras. In hindsight, we should have muted the TV or turned off the movie.

After watching the movie, we began our family devotions. While reading the Bible, we heard the bathroom closet door slam loudly. I told my family to sit tight because we often have distractions when we do family devotions. At times, the annoyances cause us to laugh because they are quite predictable. I call it spiritual harassment and believe that it seeks to distract us from our encounter with God as we meditate upon his word.

After the devotional, I went to investigate the source of the noise. I discovered that the linen closet door was fully open and the contents were strewn all over the floor. Additionally, three fire alarms near the bathroom were twisted off the brackets that held them to the ceiling. They hung by their wires. Even worse, I was attacked by the spirits. Once again, my chest began to hurt badly. I stumbled out to my family. My wife looked at my ashen face and knew I was hurting. When I came out, the demons also attacked her. In that crazy moment, my daughter stood up to help me. When she did, she became very dizzy and began to shake. We had to hold her to keep her from crashing to the ground. In a few moments, everything went wild.

At this point, I did a mini-exorcism of myself and my startled family. Self-deliverance is an important life skill for those who do spiritual warfare. Then we closed the spiritual door by repenting that we allowed the movie to be played in our home and we rededicated our house to Jesus Christ. Then I prayed over the bathroom area. An important lesson was learned. Movies can open spiritual doors in your home, especially movies that include prayers to false gods or portray evil or occult content.

Around this time, I began the practice of going into my backyard at night to commune with God on my prayer stump. Normally, this is a time of private meditation and worship. Sitting under the canopy of heaven inspires me. I love to look up at the stars and worship God. I first developed this practice when I was stationed in Iraq. When you live outside, you learn to become attuned to God in nature.

On this night, I sensed an inner desire to declare Jesus' lordship as I peered into the night sky with uplifted arms. I felt intensely anointed as I boldly magnified Jesus' name and proclaimed my allegiance to him and his kingdom. Hubris got the best of me. I made the mistake of speaking directly to the powers and principalities when I pronounced their defeat, proclaimed God's judgment on them, and claimed my city for Jesus.

As I spoke into the night, I heard a branch snap about twenty-five yards from me. Inwardly, I knew what was about to happen. From across the yard, the broken branch flew at me and hit my face. Fortunately, I was wearing my glasses. I laughed at the attack and told the demons that it would take more than a stick to make me quiet. Still, the bleeding cut on my face reminded me that Satan takes warfare prayer seriously and that caution is recommended. It is one thing to command ground level demons when casting them out of a person. It is another to confront the cosmic powers. Lesson learned: do not go beyond your authority or your covering.

More Audacious Attacks

Things in the house came to a head in early May of 2014. When I came home for lunch, a friend who was refurbishing our guest bathroom came out to see me. When she did, everything on one of the living room shelves flew three feet and fell on the floor. The shelf did not move. Obviously, this greatly alarmed her. Frantically, she began to pick up the broken things and return them to the shelf. I told her to leave them alone. With hesitation, she returned to the bathroom to resume her work.

In a few moments, she yelled my name in panic. When I reached her, she pointed to the linen closet and said that something was making a hissing noise. When I opened the door, a new can of shaving cream twisted in circles as it squirted foam all over the closet. I grabbed the can, covered the hole with my thumb, and buried it at the bottom of the garage trash can. When I returned to the living room, the water garden by the front door made a loud noise and began to shoot a geyser of water high into the air. Needless to say, my friend screamed in terror.[8]

---

8. The haunting that I describe in my home is not as uncommon as some imagine. As I write this section, the national news just reported a similar haunting at the childhood home of serial killer, Ted Bundy. According to Glenn, unsuspecting workers who were attempting to remodel Bundy's former home were bombarded with a litany of demonic hindrances. "One time [when] they re-entered the house, which had been locked, [they found] that every cabinet was open. He said one worker spotted the words 'Help me' scrawled across a basement window and while the crew was working downstairs they heard a dresser in the upstairs hallway fall. Cellphones and other electronics would also occasionally get unplugged and immediately die." (Glenn, "Eerie things going on at serial killer's childhood home in Tacoma," para. 24). Additionally, a recently declassified CIA report about a house haunting declares that, "The poltergeist manifested itself over the years in well-known uniform patterns: beds were moved about, pillows and covers were pulled off, locked doors were inexplicably opened, the contents of cupboards were

Section One: What I Didn't Learn In Seminary

The following Thursday, I taught an evening class. Before the class began, I went to a private place to pray. While I was praying, evil spirits attacked again. This attack was more severe than the others. My chest hurt, I couldn't breathe, and I gagged for air. Something was choking me. In desperation, I cried out to God for help. I pleaded that I was only a mortal and couldn't win this constant battle if he didn't intervene. In a matter of moments, God acted and gave me the victory.

When I returned to my class, the students could see my red eyes and the look on my face. I may have had visible marks on my neck. Without me saying a word, some began to pray for me. One of the students participated in the Amazon prayer group. When she saw my face, she understood the problem and came forward to pray over me. Afterward, I felt vindicated. God finally intervened with power.

The next morning, I reclined on the daybed in our all-season room. Through the windows, I watched the birds and squirrels. Spring flooded my senses. For the first time in a long time, I felt deep peace. It was the peace of victory. As I meditated, I asked God what had happened the night before. He spoke to me and said, "He who the Son sets free is free indeed. Walk in your freedom" (John 8:36). I thought he was referring to the events from the previous night. However, the meaning was deeper and more profound than I could have imagined.

Subsequently, I discovered that I no longer struggled with spiritual warfare or my predilection to sin. Frankly, I did not sense temptation and my fallen nature had little sway over me. The presence of God was close to me. The things of God were a joy to me. A deep sense of the Divine abided with me. I had to cooperate with God, but I didn't have to fight the impulses of my fallen nature. I walked in this state of heavenly grace for a full six months. I won't say that I experienced sinless perfection.[9] However, I can affirm that I didn't commit any conscious sins.

Because of this experience, I understand why John Wesley said that sanctification was a work of grace and not the result of the will. One may

---

found to be in disorder, objects disappeared and reappeared, sounds were mimicked, penetration phenomena occurred and so on" (Dunn, "12 Million Pages of Declassified CIA Files Are Now Available Online for Everyone to View," para. 35). The CIA planned to complete psycho-diagnostic tests and in-depth psychological examinations. The plans didn't materialize because the family moved Guadalupe to escape the poltergeist. In their new surroundings they found peace, although even there they experienced strange phenomena such as rosaries falling from the sky.

9. See Wesley's "A Plain Account of Christian Perfection."

walk into a state of sanctification when one believes that God wants him to have it, seeks after God, and uses all the means of grace to include the spiritual disciplines. It isn't the result of willpower or legalistic mechanisms. It is a gift.

Learning to Surrender to God

Eventually, I re-entered the real world. During my time of peace and sanctification, I found out that my fallen nature, my wants, and my needs combined to predispose me to certain thoughts and behaviors that worked against God's perfect will for me, a will that is being restored in me through his grace. I also discovered that a fallen nature is a hard thing to rewire. It is almost impossible to gain victory over it when evil supernaturalism is energizing it. That is why inner healing is an important part of spiritual development for those who have struggled with the demonic.

Ultimately, I learned that sanctification is an ongoing process that requires continuous surrender to God. For example, two years ago, God revealed to me that I should not play Angry Birds on my phone. Actually, my wife's gentle nudging about the sin caused me to hear God's voice more clearly. I liked to play Angry Birds when I was waiting for my daughter to finish her piano lessons or had some downtime. When I sensed God's convicting Spirit, I repented and turned away from the mindless entertainment that distracted me from praying and meditating on the things of God. Some would argue that playing Angry Birds isn't a sin. I would respond by saying, it may not be a sin for you but it is for me because God has told me to give it up. In fact, God leads us away from many practices which interfere with his work in our lives.

Recently, I was listening to *The Trials of Apollo: The Hidden Oracle*[10] while driving my car. Previous novels by this author have taught me a lot about false religions, territorial spirits, ancient gods, and the way the spiritual world works. However, God emphatically checked me and told me to turn it off because it glorified Apollo. Even though my flesh wanted to hear the book, my spirit told me to submit to God. Afterward, I read a plot summary of the book and returned it to the library without listening to it. Fortunately, when God tells us to move away from something or give something up, he enables us to do it when we cooperate with him.

---

10. Riordan, *The Trials of Apollo*.

Section One: What I Didn't Learn In Seminary

Over the last eighteen months, I lived with a lot of frustration. At some point, my frustration became a generalized malaise. Even though I didn't act on it, I felt unsettled anger in my soul. A few months ago, God told me to rid myself of all anger. I rejoined that anger was a normal human emotion. I also reminded God that he gets angry. In some way, my ability to feel anger reflects my heavenly pedigree. At this point, God became firmer. He told me that my anger blocked my spiritual growth and hindered his ability to work in me. I told God that I would cooperate with him if he would take anger away from me.

Following that encounter, I didn't feel any anger. When I came home from work, I laughed with deep enjoyment as my puppy jumped all over me. Laughter began to dominate my life. While driving, I practiced the presence of God and didn't focus on my frustration. I also let God give me patience with others. The issues that caused me to feel discouragement didn't change. However, I tried to focus on God instead of my external issues.

Then it happened. One night, while praying under the stars in my backyard, I realized that I had deep joy in my soul. I cannot describe the feeling of being fully content. As I meditated on this, I also realized that love oozed from my soul. God is love. When one is remade in God's image, that person will love like God loves. Since love defines God, it should also define the children of God. When a believer learns to walk in love, anger can be a fleeting response to external sin but it cannot dominate the believer.

Obviously, I didn't make myself love or rid myself of my anger. One can't actualize the fruit of the Spirit through a legalistic approach (Gal 5: 22–23). The love that I felt came to me as a gift from God. In order for me to receive that precious present, I had to give up my anger. God knew what he wanted to do in my life and how he wanted to achieve it.

At this point, Christians can learn a lesson from Islam. During the years of its rapid spread, militarism and violence characterized Islam. The fight against the enemies of God was called jihad. Just like today, Muslims of different perspectives killed each other as quickly as they killed the infidels. For example, three of the first caliphs were murdered by zealous Muslims. Even Muhammed's son-in-law and grandson were killed by Muslims. Anger, violence, revenge, and intolerance dominated parts of the movement.

By the eleventh century, some Muslim sages realized that too much focus on external combat destroys the spiritual core of the Muslim revelation. As such, they began to distinguish between the lesser jihad and the greater jihad. The lesser jihad is external conflict. It fights for the way of

Allah. The greater jihad is the struggle to surrender the self to God and live at peace with him.[11] The fight against oneself is the greatest fight. All people must learn how to die to self so that they can live for God.

In the Christians life, an emphasis on spiritual warfare must be tempered by an equal emphasis on spiritual growth and self-surrender. Paul understood this truth. He admonished the saints to put on the armor of God so that they could fight against the kingdom of Satan (Eph 6:10–17). The war against the devil and his evil minions is real. Like deputized servants of God, the believers must fight against the spiritual powers, rulers, and principalities who seek to overturn the work of God and bring the world into captivity.

Paul also uses warfare language to describe how the believer is called to win the struggle against the fallen nature. For example, in 1 Timothy 6, fighting the good fight requires the overcoming believer to flee from quarrels, envy, strife, malicious talk, evil suspicions, and constant friction between people of corrupt mind who think that godliness is a means to financial gain. Instead, they are to strive for righteousness, godliness, faith, love, endurance, and gentleness. In short, learning to crucify the flesh and walk in the Spirit also qualifies as spiritual warfare (Gal 5:24–25).

I close this section with a quote from James. "Submit yourselves, then, to God. Resist the devil, and he will flee from you. Come near to God and he will come near to you. Wash your hands, you sinners, and purify your hearts, you double-minded" (4:7–8). All spiritual warfare begins with an act of surrendering to God.

---

11. Crim et al, "Jihad," 381–382.

Section Two

Spiritually Equipped For Anointed Ministry

4

The Disciples Are Equipped to Do Anointed Ministry

THE GOSPELS PAINT A striking picture of a miracle-working, gospel preaching Messiah who destroys the kingdom of Satan as he inaugurates the long-expected reign of God. In dramatic fashion, messengers from John the Baptist ask Jesus, "Are you the one who is to come, or should we expect someone else?" (Luke 7:19). While the messengers wait for a response, Jesus heals the sick, gives sight to the blind, cleanses the lepers, casts out demons, and raises a dead child. After performing all these miracles, he doesn't give John's messenger a yes or no answer. Instead, he tells them, "Go back and report to John what you have seen and heard: The blind receive sight, the lame walk, those who have leprosy are cleansed, the deaf hear, the dead are raised, and the good news is proclaimed to the poor" (Luke 7:22).[1]

According to Luke's gospel, Jesus' ministry proved that he was the Messiah because it fulfilled messianic prophecy, destroyed Satan's kingdom, and unveiled God's kingdom on earth. John's gospel makes a similar point. When the opponents of Jesus pressed Jesus to say that he was the

---

1. John the Baptist and his disciples anticipated that Jesus would bring political liberation when he inaugurated the Day of the Lord. Jesus' lack of political engagement confused them. Previously, in Luke 4:17–19, Jesus quoted from Isaiah to announce his messiahship. "The Spirit of the Lord is on me, because he has anointed me to proclaim good news to the poor. He has sent me to proclaim freedom for the prisoners and recovery of sight for the blind, to set the oppressed free, to proclaim the year of the Lord's favor." John and his disciples would have interpreted this verse in light of Roman oppression. However, instead of freeing the Jews from Roman rule, Jesus frees them from Satan and his malice. His miracles show that he is pushing back the kingdom of darkness.

Messiah so they would have cause to stone him, Jesus told them that his works proved that he was the Messiah. Even if they didn't believe his words when he said that he was the Messiah, his power ministry showed that he came from the Father. Furthermore, the miracles that he performed testified that he was God's Son. That truth was incontrovertible. For that reason, their opposition to him was unmerited (John 5:36 and 10:22–38). In all the gospels, Jesus' power ministry reveals the kingdom of God and shows that he is the Messiah.

In the context of the in-breaking kingdom, a church that doesn't do power ministry cannot say that it is walking in the stead of Christ. Powerless Christianity is an oxymoron and an obstacle to God's redemptive purposes! Jesus anticipated this problem. That is why he prepared his disciples to expand his kingdom by equipping them to do the same works that he did. Not only did he show them how to do his work, he told them that they would do greater works than he did because he was going to the Father (John 14:12). From his exalted position in heaven, he would anoint them with the Holy Spirit and give them spiritual power so they could increase his work.

Matthew 8 and 9 present an action-packed, power ministry narrative that sets the stage for the commissioning of the disciples. The narrative ends with a summary statement that is a bookend to Matthew 4:23–25. It says, "Jesus went through all the towns and villages, teaching in their synagogues, proclaiming the good news of the kingdom and healing every disease and sickness. When he saw the crowds, he had compassion on them, because they were harassed and helpless, like sheep without a shepherd. Then he said to his disciples, 'The harvest is plentiful but the workers are few. Ask the Lord of the harvest, therefore, to send out workers into his harvest field'" (Matt 9:35–38).

In answer to his prayer request, Jesus sets apart the twelve apostles, empowers them to do his work, and sends them into the harvest (Matt 10:1–16). He is the Lord of the harvest. When he sends them out, he gives them additional instructions. They are to proclaim the good news of the kingdom as they cure the sick, raise the dead, cleanse the lepers, and cast out the demons (10:7). Their ministry instructions match the summary statement of Jesus' ministry in Matthew 9:35–38. In other words, Jesus dispatches the apostles to mass produce his ministry all over Galilee.

Lest we think that the ministry to cast out demons and heal the sick was only given to the twelve apostles, Luke adds that Jesus sent out an additional

The Disciples Are Equipped to Do Anointed Ministry

seventy disciples with similar instructions (Luke 10:1–12). They were to go into the towns and villages that Jesus intended to visit and prepare the crowds for his arrival by preaching and doing power ministry. When the seventy returned from their mission (Luke 10:17–20), they rejoiced because the demons had to submit to them when they invoked Jesus' name (v.17).

Trained to Do Power Ministry

In the gospels, the disciples shared Jesus' authority and did his work because he deputized them for that work. Additionally, one must assume that Jesus taught them how to do what he did before he sent them out. That is what teachers do. The Scriptures show that Jesus taught the disciples how to pray (Luke 11:1). Later, when they couldn't cast out a demon, the disciples asked him why they couldn't do what he taught them how to do. His answer provided additional training (Matt 17:17–19). The apostles were so accustomed to taking advantage of every learning opportunity that Peter asked Jesus to command him to walk on the water when he realized that Jesus was walking on the water (Matt 14:28). If Jesus could do it, Peter assumed that he could do it. When he failed, Jesus corrected him by telling him what he did wrong. In this case, he lost faith when he took his eyes off Jesus and looked at the waves.[2]

If today's church had more spiritual warfare practitioners who trained novices, power ministry would be more common. For example, a person from Latin America recently called me and asked me to pray for her stomach. Previously, God had enabled me to cast out some very recalcitrant demons from her and bring healing to her body. She calls me when she needs a word from God or advice. I sensed that she had become dependent. This time I refused to pray for her. Instead, I instructed her how to pray for herself. When she did, God gave her the healing she desired. She was overjoyed. Now, she knows how to minister to herself and others.

Two years ago, I was teaching at a seminary in Colombia. One night a person sent me a computer message on Facebook. I had met the person when I was ministering in Costa Rica. As we typed, things got strange. Finally, I asked her to call me. During the call, I had to confront some very

---

2. People called Jesus rabbi because he was a teacher. In addition to power ministry, Jesus also taught his disciples how to forgive sins, how to do communion, and how to love each other. Even though the Bible doesn't give the details, one can assume that Jesus trained his disciples to do everything that he did.

vociferous demons who continued to manifest even after I commanded them to go down. The woman was terrified. Since I wasn't making progress, I told the woman to follow my instructions as I walked her through self-deliverance. At first, it was very tense because the demons kept trying to take over. However, within thirty minutes, the woman had cast out the afflicting demons and was able to receive counseling from me. As a matter of practice, I always teach people how to do self-deliverance after I minister inner healing to them.[3]

Last year, the Lord touched my daughter in a special way. Since then, her mother and I have witnessed words of knowledge come from her at unexpected times. For example, during family devotions, I shared that God had given me a vision for a person. Since I felt a burden for the person, I shared the vision. Without hesitation, my daughter gave me a detailed interpretation of the vision. I knew her words were true because God confirmed them to me. The interpretation enabled me to minister effectively to the person for whom God gave me the vision.

After my daughter gave me the spontaneous and very precise interpretation, I asked her how she knew the meaning of the vision. She replied, "I don't know. It just came to me. It felt right." Since then, I have been helping her develop that gifting. I truly believe that most Christians are gifted for some level of supernatural ministry. Moreover, I believe that Jesus did the same thing with his apostles. Bottom-line; if you have a special ministry gifting, you should teach someone else how to do what you do. Pass it on!

Interestingly, between the crucifixion of Jesus and the giving of the Holy Spirit on the Day of Pentecost, the Bible doesn't record that the disciples engaged in any power ministry. It appears that they were powerless during this time. Why? They couldn't do power ministry because the power anointing that they enjoyed due to their proximity to Jesus was no longer available to them. Since they could no longer share his anointing, they needed their own anointing.

That is why Jesus explicitly told them not to go anywhere or try to do anything until they received the power of the Holy Spirit. Specifically, Jesus said, "Do not leave Jerusalem, but wait for the gift my Father promised, which you have heard me speak about. For John baptized with water, but in a few days you will be baptized with the Holy Spirit" (Acts 1:5–6). They weren't equipped to pursue the global mission of being his witnesses from

---

3. Derek Prince offers guidelines for doing self-deliverance. See *They Shall Expel Demons*, 203–218.

Jerusalem unto the ends of the earth until they received divine power (Acts 1:8). That power was given to them when they were baptized with the Holy Spirit on the Day of Pentecost.

Jesus Needed Spirit-Baptism

Ironically, the God-with-us man who baptizes with the Holy Spirit also needed to be baptized with the Holy Spirit in order to embark on his God-given mission. John the Baptist declares this when he says, "I saw the Spirit come down from heaven as a dove and remain on him. And I myself did not know him, but the one who sent me to baptize with water told me, 'The man on whom you see the Spirit come down and remain is the one who will baptize with the Holy Spirit'" (John 1:32–33).

When Jesus became human, he emptied himself of his divine right (Phil 2:6–8). In the incarnation, Jesus didn't cease to be God. Rather, in order to be fully human, he laid down his divine attributes. That is why the temptation story represented a series of real temptations. It is also why Jesus really died when he was crucified. A spirit being that animates a human body isn't a real human. Jesus knew who he was. Even though he had access to his full divinity, he chose to bury it so he could live like any other human being. In truth, Jesus had to empty himself to become a real human because mortal people aren't all-powerful beings who know all things and can be in all places at the same time.

Because Jesus was a real man who emptied himself of his divine right when he was incarnated, he needed to be baptized with the Holy Spirit to do power ministry. In support of this, the canonical gospels don't report that Jesus did any miracles before his baptism. The twelve-year-old Jesus who talked with the elders in the Temple (Luke 2:41–52) was aware of his identity but didn't act on it until he was baptized with the Holy Spirit.

The Disciples Are Spirit-filled So They Can Accomplish the Mission of God

The implications of the above truth are enormous for Christ-disciples who are called and sent into the world to minister on Jesus' behalf. If Jesus couldn't accomplish the Father's work without Spirit-baptism and if the apostles couldn't do power ministry until they were filled with the Spirit on Pentecost, how can modern disciples continue Christ's work in the world without being filled with the Spirit? This is the reason that Jesus told the disciples to wait until they were baptized with the Holy Spirit before they set off on their mission. They needed the power that comes from divine anointing.

When seen from this perspective, the Spirit-baptism on the Day of Pentecost was the way God empowered the gathered disciples to accomplish his mission. The immediate aftermath shows this. When the crowds came to investigate the commotion of Pentecost, a powerfully anointed Peter preached a stirring gospel message to the assembled crowd so that some 3,000 Jews from all over the world believed the gospel and received Christ. Furthermore, between the Day of Pentecost and the great persecution that broke out against the Jerusalem Church in Acts 8, signs and wonders, powerful preaching, exponential membership growth, and discipleship training characterized the church's ministry. In fact, hordes brought their sick and those tormented by impure spirits to the church. Acts states that all of them were healed. As a result, more and more Jews believed in the Lord Jesus and were added to the church daily (5:14–16). This clearly demonstrates the positive relationship between power ministry and church growth.

Without a doubt, the great persecution that followed the stoning of Stephen in Acts 7 ignited a global mission.[4] When the church members scattered to the four winds, some returned to their homes and seeded new congregations in faraway places. Others preached the gospel, planted churches, and furthered the missionary expansion of the church. All who fled from Jerusalem took the gospel to new places (Acts 11:19–20).

---

4. Following the Pentecost outpouring, the apostles and the members of the Jerusalem Church stayed in Jerusalem and didn't pursue the global mandate that Christ gave to them before he ascended. Most likely, they lingered in Jerusalem because they thought that Christ would return quickly and set up an earthly kingdom. The words that Jesus spoke after the Last Supper on the night before he died could imply this. In that conversation, Jesus told the apostles that he would confer a kingdom on them so they could judge the twelve tribes of Israel and sit at his table in his kingdom (Luke 22:29–30). In Matthew 19:28, this event is fulfilled after the second coming of Jesus. Because the apostles expected the imminent return of Christ, they asked Jesus if he was going to restore the kingdom before he ascended (Acts 1:6). As further verification that they expected a literal kingdom of God on earth in their lifetime, immediately after Jesus returned to heaven the apostles replaced Judas because there had to be twelve apostles to sit on twelve thrones. Also, following the ascension, the church didn't understand that the global evangelistic mandate included the Gentiles. In keeping with the Day of Pentecost example, they thought that Jesus intended the global outreach to target the Hellenistic Jews who lived among the nations. Probably, they expected that Jews from all over the world would return to Jerusalem, be converted, and seed the soon-to-be-realized Messianic kingdom over which they would reign with Christ.

The Disciples Are Equipped to Do Anointed Ministry

This truth has caused some to muse that God used the persecution to propel the church into the Gentile world. Before Acts 8, God gathered Jewish believers from all over the world to the Jerusalem Church so that they could sit under the anointed teaching of the apostles. During this formative time, God didn't allow the Jerusalem Church to be scattered because the new saints weren't ready to carry Jesus to the world.

Think of it this way. People from all over the world joined the Jerusalem Church in Acts 2. While participating in that church community, they were Spirit-filled, nurtured in the faith, and prepared for ministry. From Acts 2 to the time of the scattering in Acts 8, an international army of prophets, evangelists, pastors, teachers, and highly anointed believers received training that equipped them to accomplish the apostolic mission of the church in the world. This was the boot camp era of the church. The rest of Acts chronicles the global advance of the church and the ensuing war against Satan in accordance with the progression given by Jesus in Acts 1:8. "But you will receive power when the Holy Spirit comes on you; and you will be my witnesses in Jerusalem, and in all Judea and Samaria, and to the ends of the earth."

As he fled, Phillip the Evangelist preached the gospel in Samaria and performed supernatural signs and wonders that validated the gospel and showed that Jesus was more powerful than any other god. As a result, the people of Samaria turned from their sorcery, accepted Christ, and received the baptism of the Holy Spirit (Acts 8:17). After that, an angel directed Phillip to evangelize the Ethiopian eunuch who was transporting an Isaiah scroll back to the Ethiopian Jews (Acts 8:26–39). Many believe that this man planted the church in Ethiopia after Phillip evangelized him.

Next, God sent Peter to preach to a God-fearing Roman Army official and his associates. These Gentiles supported Judaism but weren't Jewish proselytes. When Peter preached to them, God filled them with the Holy Spirit and gave them the gift of tongues (Acts 10:44–46). Afterward, unnamed disciples who had been scattered because of the persecution came to Antioch and began to evangelize run-of-the-mill people who had no relationship with Judaism or Christianity. As a result, a great number of Gentiles became believers and turned to the Lord. When Barnabas came to check out the revival in Antioch, he found a spiritually gifted church (Acts 11:19–26). Finally, missionary bands took the gospel all over Asia Minor, Europe, northern Africa, and Mesopotamia. In fact, the Apostle Thomas went as far as India. Originally, he went to evangelize a large settlement of

Jews in Kerala. Eventually, he was martyred by a Brahmin priest because he boldly preached the gospel to the Indians.

This incredible story shows how Spirit-baptism can empower normal people to do extraordinary things. In fact, a ragtag band of fishermen, tax collectors, soldiers, mothers, merchants, zealots, and a former Pharisee took the gospel to the ends of the earth (from Spain all the way to India) within fifty years of the death of Jesus. I believe that their global advance was more impressive than that of Alexander the Great because the Christians missionaries had no army or government establishment to support them. Instead, they accomplished their work through the power of the Holy Spirit that filled them, anointed them, and equipped them for ministry.

God still bestows the same Spirit that animated and empowered the early missionaries. Peter proclaimed the universality of Spirit-baptism when he said, "Repent and be baptized, every one of you, in the name of Jesus Christ for the forgiveness of your sins. And you will receive the gift of the Holy Spirit. The promise is for you and your children and for all who are far off—for all whom the Lord our God will call" (Acts 2:38–39).

Even though Americans are "far off" in time and distance, God rekindled the Pentecostal fire in their midst. The first flickers of the coming fire began in 1901 at Topeka Bible School. During a subsequent revival in Los Angeles from 1906–1915, unnumbered masses of spiritually hungry people came to be filled and empowered by the Holy Spirit. Like the disciples on the Day of Pentecost, they received the baptism of the Holy Spirit and spoke in tongues. Many claim that it represents the rebirth of apostolic Christianity. Afterward, energized believers spread the new/old faith all over America. Others took it to the ends of the earth. Ensuing waves of revival and Holy Spirit outpourings have reshaped global Christianity. Although Christians in Latin America, Africa, and Asia represent many denominations, the majority have one thing in common. They are Spirit-filled and charismatic in their orientation.

5

Gifted for Mission and Ministry

"Now you are the body of Christ, and each one of you is a part of it. And God has placed in the church first of all apostles, second prophets, third teachers, then miracles, then gifts of healing, of helping, of guidance, and of different kinds of tongues. Are all apostles? Are all prophets? Are all teachers? Do all work miracles? Do all have gifts of healing? Do all speak in tongues? Do all interpret?" (1 Cor 12:28–30).

The organization of an ant colony illustrates how the body of Christ operates as one body with many members. Biological design determines how ants are equipped to accomplish their work. A queen produces eggs, drones mate with the queen, nannies care for the eggs, soldiers fight off invaders, foragers gather food, and workers maintain the nest. A successful colony may steal eggs from other colonies. When the pilfered eggs hatch, they become slave ants. An individual ant does not live for itself. Instead, each exists for the sake of the greater good. In a strange way, the colony is one organism composed of a multitude of individual ants. Because every type of ant is essential for the survival of the group and the accomplishment of its purpose, some force of nature must ensure that the colony has the right mix of ants. Too many or too few of any kind of ant will doom the colony.

Like the ant colony, the church is one body with many members. Within the organic whole, the Holy Spirit forms individual members into specific body parts by means of gifting them for a particular service. When a person is born again, the new believer is like a human stem cell. The person can become any part of the body. God decides what part the person will become when God assigns the individual a task in the body. Tasks equal ministry function. Paul speaks to this when he says that the Holy Spirit distributes gifts to the various members of the body (1 Cor 12:11).

God has designed the body of Christ so that gifted individuals are grafted into local communities of faith where they use their gifts in conjunction with the other spiritually gifted members of that church. Like an ant colony, each community of faith must have the right mix of gifts. For this reason, when contemplating spiritual gifts, the point of reference is the church (body of Christ), not the gifted individual (member) because God gifts an individual with the community of faith in mind.

This is why Paul focuses on the whole body rather than the individual members when he discusses how the church is shaped for ministry and mission. "Just as a body, though one, has many parts, but all its many parts form one body, so it is with Christ. For we were all baptized by one Spirit so as to form one body—whether Jews or Gentiles, slave or free—and we were all given the one Spirit to drink. Even so the body is not made up of one part but of many" (1 Cor 12:12–14).

In sum, a human body without arms would be handicapped and an arm without a body would be useless. In the same way, a spiritual body without the right assortment of gifted members wouldn't be able to function well. Gifted believers need to use their gifts in tandem with the local church and local churches need to be filled with a variety of gifted members.

Contrary to what some believe, God has not fixed a spiritual hierarchy within the church that says that some Christians are more important than others or that some spiritual gifts are more important than other spiritual gifts. Instead, when seen from the perspective of the whole, every spiritual gift and every believer is of equal value. Allow me to re-emphasize this point. A believer's worth is not determined by the spiritual gifts that the person exercises. Rather, believers should draw their identity and self-worth from Christ, not the gifts that they manifest. In light of this truth, it is essential that every believer identifies how the Holy Spirit has shaped him for ministry so that the person can develop his gift and mesh his gifting into the whole.

Old Testament Examples of People Being Filled with the Spirit for Special Tasks

The previous chapter showed how the baptism of the Holy Spirit prepared Jesus and the New Testament church for ministry and mission. Some have suggested that Spirit-baptism only existed in the New Testament and that it isn't needed today. However, a closer look at Scripture shows that Spirit-baptism is needed today because it is how God has always enabled people to complete ministry tasks.

The Old Testament offers many examples of people being filled with the Spirit. For example, Moses was filled with the Spirit when God commissioned him to go to Egypt. Afterward, the power of God flowed through him as he performed signs and wonders. While the Hebrews wandered in the wilderness, the many tasks became too great for Moses. Out of kindness to Moses, God separated seventy elders from the people so they could share his burden. To seal the deal, God poured on them a portion of the Spirit that he had previously given to Moses (Num 11:16-17). As an external manifestation that they had received the Spirit, the elders prophesied one time (v 25). When the people heard them prophesying, they knew that God had anointed them for the ministry.

Additionally, in the same way that Peter and John laid hands on the Samaritan believers so that they received the Holy Spirit (Acts 8:14-17), Moses put his hands on Joshua so he would receive the Holy Spirit. When he did, Moses imparted the gift of wisdom to him. Because of this, the people gladly followed Joshua after Moses died (Deut 34:9). King Solomon also received the gift of wisdom when he prayed for it (1Kgs 3:10-13). However, no one in the Old Testament was filled with the Spirit to the same extent as Moses (Deut 34:12).

Exodus 31:2-6 and 35:30—36:2 show that God filled other Old Testament figures with spiritual gifts to do divine tasks as craftsmen. Even though the gift of craftsmanship doesn't appear on any New Testament gift list, it was very important in the Old Testament because God needed to build a tabernacle. Whenever God needs to do something, he calls and gifts people so he can accomplish his work through them.

> See, I have chosen Bezalel son of Uri, the son of Hur, of the tribe of Judah, and I have filled him with the Spirit of God, with wisdom, with understanding, with knowledge and with all kinds of skills—to make artistic designs for work in gold, silver and bronze, to cut and set stones, to work in wood, and to engage in all kinds of crafts. Moreover, I have appointed Oholiab son of Ahisamak, of the tribe of Dan, to help him. Also I have given ability to [i.e., gifted] all the skilled workers to make everything I have commanded you (Exod 3:12-6).

Section Two: Spiritually Equipped For Anointed Ministry

The Spirit also came upon Samson in Judges 14:6 and 15:4. Even after his hair was cut off, God came upon him once more so he could complete his task as a judge to deliver the people from Philistine oppression (Judges 16:28–30). One can assume that God filled other judges and prophets with the Spirit. For example, God imparted the Spirit of the Lord, justice, power, and might to Micah so he could declare God's word to Israel (Mic 3:8). Daniel had the gift of wisdom, knowledge, interpretation of dreams, and leadership (Dan 1:17). Jews who composed the school of the prophets attended to the needs of national prophets like Elijah and Elisha. Often, they were overcome by the Spirit and prophesied as they went along.

When Saul was chosen to be the king of Israel, Samuel gave him instructions about his pending in-filling with the Spirit. "You will meet a procession of prophets coming down from the high place with lyres, timbrels, pipes and harps being played before them, and they will be prophesying. The Spirit of the Lord will come powerfully upon you, and you will prophesy with them; and you will be changed into a different person" (1 Sam 10:5–6). It happened just like Samuel said.

Sometimes God poured out his Spirit in a humorous way. When Saul sent his troops to capture David, the Spirit fell upon them and they prophesied. This happened three times. Finally, when Saul went to find out why his troops didn't return, the Spirit fell on him with such force that he prophesied all night long. He couldn't stop (1 Sam 19:18–24).

David was anointed with the Spirit when he composed divine music (2 Tim 3:16). Much of that is preserved in the Psalms. When evil spirits tormented Saul, David drove them away by playing his praise music (1 Sam 16:23). David was self-aware that he was filled with the Holy Spirit. He was also aware that God could take it from him. After his sin with Bathsheba, he asked God not to take the Holy Spirit away from him (Ps 51:11).

The prophesying that often accompanied the in-filling with the Spirit in the Old Testament is not like New Testament prophecy. In the New Testament, prophecy is a message that God gives to a person (1 Cor 14:22–25). That is, all divinely uttered prophecy contains an understandable message. On the other hand, in the Old Testament, the divine utterances of those who are filled with the Spirit do not appear to be messages for anyone. What message did Saul give when he prophesied all night long in a spiritual stupor? What divine oracles did the seventy elders utter while they were overcome by the Spirit and prophesied? I contend that the divine utterances that accompanied certain in-fillings in the Old Testament were similar to how people experience the gift of tongues today. Some would liken it to "praying in the Spirit" (1 Cor 14:15, Eph 6:18, and Jude 1:20).

Allow me to illustrate this from my personal experience. At times, God will give me a word of prophecy for another person. When he does, I get an understandable message from God. Recently, a distressed student called me. As I listened to her story, I sensed that God wanted to say something to her. "Sensed" isn't the right word. I felt words. As I began to speak, the Holy Spirit gave me a message for her. I didn't think about the words or control what was being said. I merely let the Spirit flow. In some sense, I emptied myself so the Holy Spirit could take control. The student received exactly what God wanted her to receive.

In some ways, speaking in tongues is different; in other ways, it is the same. When I speak in tongues, I never control when or how it will happen. Usually, the words bubble up from my soul when I am in deep worship or feeling especially anointed. Many times, words just pop out. I feel a profound release when it happens. Often, while praying over another person, I will slip into tongues or receive a prophetic word for the person. When I speak in tongues, I speak with a soft voice and avoid bringing attention to it. However, if I receive a prophetic message, I tell it to the person.

If someone asked me to speak in tongues, I couldn't do it because I don't control it. I feel the Holy Spirit in me when I speak in tongues. Still, I don't understand what is being said. Based on the above description, it is clear that most of the Old Testament examples of being filled with the Spirit were more like tongues than New Testament prophecy.

I know that there is a demonic counterfeit to tongues.[1] I have witnessed it. One friend checks for demonic counterfeits. He will say, "Spirit talking in tongues, do you confess that Jesus Christ is Lord and that he came in the flesh?" If he doesn't get the correct answer, he knows that the tongues are demonic. Recently, when doing an exorcism with a person who thought she spoke in tongues, the person began to speak in a counterfeit tongue. This happened many times. Finally, I rebuked the spirit and the person lost the ability to speak in tongues. Sadly, many people who have the counterfeit gift of tongues don't realize it.

---

1. The Old Testament also shows the counterfeit gift of prophesying. For example, the prophets of Ba'al continued in their "frantic prophesying" for eight hours while on Mount Carmel. The ecstatic utterances showed spirit possession and were accompanied by self-mutilation and dancing before the gods (1 Kgs 18:29).

SECTION TWO: SPIRITUALLY EQUIPPED FOR ANOINTED MINISTRY

The Night I Spoke in Tongues

I was born again in 1972 while reading Hal Lindsey's *The Late Great Planet Earth*.[2] The book spoke about the end times. It presented the plan of salvation as a way to escape from the horrors of God's impending judgment. Like those who heard John the Baptist warn the crowds to "flee from the wrath to come," I felt intense conviction when I read Lindsey's book. I prayed the sinner's prayer every day for months. As time went on, I spent long hours praying in the woods and in other private places seeking peace for my troubled soul.

God answered my prayers in the summer of 1975. On a Sunday morning before going to Church, I was reading from Billy Graham's *Peace with God*.[3] As I read a certain part, God flooded my soul with the assurance of salvation. A deep peace engulfed my being. My angst and doubt left me. For months, I basked in the joy of that experience. In retrospect, I liken it to John Wesley's Aldersgate experience. His profound encounter with God forever changed his life and sparked the great Methodist revival.

Even though I didn't know about Pentecostals when I received the assurance of salvation, my reading of the Bible convinced me that believers could be filled with the Holy Spirit. As I quested for the baptism of the Holy Spirit, I soon discovered Oral Roberts and the Full Gospel Fellowship. When I read the testimonies of people who were filled with the Holy Spirit, my soul longed for it. More importantly, I was desperate for more of God.

In 1977, I started an after-school job with *El Noticiero*, a local Cuban newspaper. My boss, Justo Hugo Venegas, was a kind man who supported my spirituality. One night while working late, I met his wife. She pastored a Pentecostal church close to my house. With her encouragement, I began to attend her services. After a few months, the desire to be baptized with the Holy Spirit became so intense that the congregation called a special service for me. They called it a tarrying service.

On the appointed night, people surrounded me as I prayed at the altar. I don't remember what anyone said. At some point, I fell backward and was "slain in the spirit." I lay motionless for a long time. As I rested in the Spirit, the service continued without me. When I came to, I was singing in tongues. I didn't know the language or the song. After thirty minutes, the pastor asked me to share my testimony. Still, I could only babble in divine

---

2. Lindsey, *The Late Great Planet Earth*.
3. Graham, *Peace with God*.

utterances. My ability to speak English was taken from me. After the service, I drove home singing in tongues. Somehow, I made it past my curious parents and into my bedroom. I don't remember anything else.

Recently, my little brother reminded me about that night. We shared bunk beds. Vividly, he described what happened. I entered the room speaking softly in tongues. I couldn't stop. Like Saul, I spoke in divine utterances all night long. At some point, before I drove us to school, I regained my ability to speak English.

Over the years, I have witnessed many people receive the baptism of the Holy Spirit. Sometimes it falls spontaneously when the person isn't expecting it. At other times, it comes to a person who is seeking it. I have seen young children and senior citizens receive the baptism of the Spirit. Now and then, the Spirit will fall on many people at one time. John the Baptist was filled with the Spirit in his mother's womb. He manifested it when he leaped at the salutation of Mary. There is no one way in which the Spirit falls on a person.

The Night My Youth Minister Spoke in Tongues

In 1998, I pastored a United Methodist Church. During our annual conference in Lakeland, Florida, the bishop from the Cuban Methodist Conference preached to the assembled pastors. Previously, the entire Cuban Methodist Church was immersed in a Holy Spirit revival. Afterward, power ministry characterized the Methodist Church in Cuba. The Cuban bishop concluded his sermon with an altar call in which he invited the pastors to come forward and receive a ministry anointing.

At my urging, my youth pastor attended the service. She was new to the ministry. Previously, she had never heard of the baptism of the Holy Spirit. However, she desired to know God and was hungry for a closer walk. We went to the altar call at the bishop's bidding. Nothing happened to her even though God touched others.

While driving home at 1:00 am, she called me on my cell phone. I could tell that something was wrong because she sounded frightened. As she drove down backcountry roads in the middle of nowhere, she was listening to praise music. In time, she lost herself in worship and praise. At some point, she realized that she was speaking in a language that she didn't know. With gasps, she asked me what was happening to her. I told her to turn off the praise music, open the windows, and drive home with both hands on the steering wheel. I promised to tell her all about it in the morning.

After this, she became a powerful minister. With the help of a group of like-minded women, she grew a large children's and youth program. In time, the youth ministry swelled to seventy-five students and included a great praise band. It began to have its own worship services on Sunday morning. This led to home prayer groups. Eventually, a revival broke out among the youth. Many were filled with the Holy Spirit and transformed. Without the youth minister's spiritual leadership, none of that would have happened.

Global Pentecostalism

Do I believe that my youth pastor was a born-again child of God before the Holy Spirit fell on her? Yes, I do. Do I believe that the world is filled with wonderfully gifted Christians who don't speak in tongues, people who have anointed ministries? Yes, I do. Do I believe that all Spirit-filled believers speak in tongues? No, I don't (1 Cor 12:30). Do I believe that most of the examples of Spirit-baptism in the New Testament include the evidence of speaking in tongues? Yes, I do.[4]

When I lived in Central London, I often attended Holy Trinity Brompton Anglican Church. It is the mother church of the Alpha Course. The secular people who attend the Alpha Course participate in a Holy Spirit weekend. During that weekend, the participants learn about the Spirit. Additionally, most are filled with the Spirit. When speaking about the baptism of the Spirit, the leaders distinguish between having the Spirit and being filled with the Spirit. Even though all Christians have the Spirit, they emphasize a lifestyle in which believers keep on being filled with the Spirit.

During the Holy Spirit weekend, people usually display a physical manifestation when they are filled with the Spirit. The manifestations may include heat flowing through the body, being slain in the Spirit, breathing deeply, or more dramatic expressions. The leaders celebrate the gift of

---

4. Before the global advent of Pentecostalism, the holiness movement emphasized that sanctification evidenced Spirit baptism. Accordingly, "Walking in the Spirit" and bearing the fruit of the Spirit indicated that God's Spirit was working in a person to transform the person into the image of Christ (Gal 5:13–26). Much of that emphasis has been lost in Pentecostalism because it focuses on gift manifestation instead of holiness.

tongues but do not believe that one must speak in them to be filled with the Spirit.[5]

Interestingly, the Methodist Pentecostal Church in Chile came into existence through a spontaneous outpouring of the Holy Spirit in 1909. People displayed many manifestations of the Spirit to include a Spirit-filled prophetess that went around declaring people's hidden sins in accordance with the teaching in 1 Corinthians 14:24–25. Even today, the Methodist Pentecostal Church is characterized by a powerful anointing. However, the church doesn't teach that everyone must speak in tongues in order to be Spirit-filled. Instead, it believes that God can give an individual any gift as evidence of the in-filling. Still, the in-filling usually comes with an external manifestation. This theology seems to be normative in much of Latin America.

In 2015, while preaching in Pentecostal Holiness churches in Costa Rica, I often asked attendees if they spoke in tongues. Most didn't. Sometimes the pastors didn't. At the same time, I discovered that people who attended non-Pentecostal churches did speak in tongues. Usually, it was hard for me to distinguish between the Pentecostal and the non-Pentecostal churches. Basically, every church I attended was Spirit-filled.[6]

When I taught in Lagos, Nigeria last year, even my Anglican students were Spirit-filled. When I commented on this, one priest exclaimed, "We are African Anglicans. We aren't like our British brothers." These African students had never visited Holy Trinity Brompton! The same is true throughout most of the global church. Being filled with the Holy Spirit has become the global norm everywhere except in Europe and the English-speaking world. As such, I feel no need to defend the Bible's emphasis on Spirit-baptism.

As I mentioned in the last chapter, since a series of global "Pentecostal" type revivals broke out in the early 1900s, people all over the world have experienced the baptism of the Holy Spirit. It has colored the face of global Christianity. In parts of Latin America, over 70 percent of the people claim to be Charismatic or Pentecostal. Being Spirit-filled is so common in the global church that it has become the norm.

---

5. See Gumbel, "Talk 11 – How Can I Be Filled with the Holy Spirit?"
6. For more information on Latino Pentecostalism, see Payne, "Folk Religion and the Pentecostal Surge in Latin America."

6

Flowing with Spiritual Gifts

As I mentioned in the Introduction, my approach to power ministry has been greatly influenced by Dr. Charles Kraft from Fuller Theological Seminary. To be closer to him, I completed a sabbatical at Fuller in the winter of 2006. To my great delight, every class that he taught began with a demonstration of power ministry. His classes were always full!

In 2003, while he and I drove to teach a class in Cleveland, Ohio, we discussed my pending course in spiritual warfare and power encounter. I felt quite nervous since I had never taught a graduate-level course on that topic. Like many professors, I understood the theory better than the practice. To ease my discomfort, Kraft reminded me of the revival at Pasadena, the Signs and Wonders class, and the beginnings of the Third Wave Movement. During that time, he and C. Peter Wagner sat under the teaching of John Wimber. At his bidding, they practiced the spiritual gifts until they learned how to flow with them. Then he gave me sound advice, "Trust the Holy Spirit. He will equip you for the class. What you are lacking, he will provide. Be prepared to flow with the Holy Spirit and he will teach you what you don't know. Above all, have fun." I refer to this as "just in time anointing."

Kraft doesn't emphasize spiritual gifts as much as Pentecostals or Charismatics because he believes that gifting is dynamic. That is, even though a person may have a primary set of spiritual gifts from which he or she operates, the Spirit will give a believer whatever gift the person needs when the person needs it in order for the person to fulfill God's mission. For example, Kraft is gifted for inner healing. He is strongly anointed in that ministry. However, while ministering God often gives him the ability to manifest other gifts like physical healing. Consequently, he says that people should be prepared to walk in any gift that God bestows upon them whenever God wants them to accomplish something.

Learning How to Flow with the Spirit

Before I taught the Power Encounter class, I prayed over the roster. While I was praying, God told me that a specific student had a gift of healing. At that point, I didn't know the students. On the first night of class, I announced that one of the students had a gift of healing and that the student would discover it during the class. I promised the students that God would reveal the gifted student before the end of the course. So that they would know that I spoke the truth, I placed a check by the student's name on my class roster.

Per the syllabus, every class had to conclude with a ministry practice session. I really didn't know how to do the practice sessions. So, I started by praying over the class. As I moved my outstretched right hand from one side to the next, I noticed that it felt hot and tingly when it pointed in the direction of a certain female student. I was curious. Was God showing me something? I became a little more intentional. As I did, the sensations became more explicit. Finally, I told the student that God wanted us to pray for her. I invited three female students to join me. As we prayed over her, my hand began to burn. I don't remember the details, but I do remember that the woman was touched by God in some specific ways for which she was in great need.

In the following weeks, the Spirit continued to show me who to pray for by means of tingling sensations and burning hands when I stood in front of the class. Additionally, when I stood in front of the person for whom I was directed to pray, God would show me which part of the body needed prayer. Specifically, my hand would get very warm when it hovered over the right spot. Moreover, even though I didn't touch the person, the person would also feel heat in the location where I prayed. Was it a sympathetic response? What did it mean?

At first, I felt tempted to doubt my discovery because the Bible doesn't say anything about warm hands and tingly sensations when you pray for someone. Then I remembered that the woman with the issue of blood felt something in her body when she was healed, and Jesus felt power go from him when he healed her (Mark 5:29–30). Although the Bible doesn't describe the sensation, it affirms that both the healer and the one being healed felt something. Furthermore, many faith healers have reported that they feel warm hands when they pray for the sick and many healed people have stated they feel radiating heat when they are touched by the Spirit. In fact, when I reported my experience to my colleagues, one stated that he felt a searing heat on his spinal cord when God healed it during a class as a group of students prayed for him.

A Student Discovers a Gift

One night the students asked if they could pray over me. When I consented, they sat me in a chair and gathered around me. Many hands were laid on me. I wore a thick leather coat because it was very cold. While they prayed, I felt a surge of heat burn through the jacket. It ran down my spinal cord. Without thinking, I reached behind me and grabbed the hot hand. The hand belonged to the student with the check by his name. His hand continued to radiate heat after I removed it from me. I asked the other students to feel it. They were astounded by the intense heat that issued from it.

When I showed the student that I had placed the check by his name before the class began, he acknowledged that God had called him to heal the sick. This revelation made him cry because he came from a Baptist background that didn't believe in the sign gifts. Additionally, an old woman in a wheelchair to whom he was ministering in a hospital had previously told him that he was gifted for healing. Even though he believed that she was a prophetess, at that time, he rejected her message to him. After denying his ministry calling for all those years, he reported that he was finally ready to own it.

He was an Army major on some type of vocational rehabilitation. During the day, he interned at the local VA Medical Center. Since the hospital didn't know what to do with him, they assigned him to the chaplain's office. After accepting his healing gift, he began to pray for veterans. To everyone's surprise, many got better. He became so popular that patients began to ask for him by name.

At one point, the mental health department summoned him. They had a long-term suicidal patient who had recently been extracted from the top of the water tower. Whenever he got out, he tried to kill himself. The unit told my student to do his thing. With that, they shut him in with the patient. Since the class had taught the students how to cast out demons, the student knew what to do. After his visit, the patient recovered and was discharged after three days.

One of the students took the class because she needed an elective. She had lost her faith, was married to an agnostic Jew, and strongly disliked Pentecostals. God strongly touched her during the class. In the aftermath, she reclaimed her faith and discovered a new joy in doing gifted ministry. Other students also discovered ministry gifts that they didn't realize they had. Everyone was spiritually uplifted as they learned to flow with the Holy Spirit in anointed ministry.

The Example of Jesus and Spiritual Gifts

According to John 3:34, God gave the Spirit to Jesus without measure. All the gifts flowed through him. During the time that the disciples itinerated with him, they had access to his anointing when they duplicated his ministry. After the Day of Pentecost, the entire church reproduced Jesus' example through the empowering of the Holy Spirit.

As was noted in the last chapter, all the gifts are present in the church in the same way that they were all present in Christ. However, no individual has all the gifts in the same way that Jesus did. In the post-Pentecost era, believers are called and gifted for the ministry that God assigns to them. Since the God-with-us Messiah returned to heaven, it is unrealistic for any individual Christian to think that he or she should do everything that Jesus did. This will come as a breath of fresh air to those who labor under the myth of the super-Christian.

Since I believe that all the gifts are potentially present in the church, I expect that I will encounter them. For that reason, I look for healings, deliverance from evil spirits, miracles of multiplication, words of knowledge, prophesy, anointed preaching, discerning of spirits, efficient administration, anointed music, and raising the dead. God is dynamic. Since the various listings of gifts in the New Testament are all different, we shouldn't assume that the New Testament intended to create a standard listing of all the available gifts. The number of potential gifts is as extensive as God is creative. I have already shown that craftsmanship is a spiritual gift even though it is not listed in the New Testament.

Furthermore, I have discovered that most people who have a calling with a corresponding spiritual gift also have a gift mix to accompany the calling. The gift mix represents specific spiritual gifts that go together. At this stage in my life, my primary calling is teaching. My gift mix includes preaching and evangelism. Often, words of knowledge and prophecy pop up when I am doing ministry. Sometimes I receive visions. Often, I do exorcisms and flow with healing.

Previously I noted that my fifteen-year-old daughter recently received the baptism of the Holy Spirit. She is still learning what her ministry calling is. Already, I have witnessed words of knowledge and interpretation of visions. When she was a young child, God sent a prophetess to us while we were in a restaurant at Natural Bridge State Park in Kentucky. She gave us a very exact message related to my daughter's calling. So that we wouldn't forget the message, we wrote it on a piece of paper. Periodically, we reread the message. I expect that my daughter will move into the ministry that God has prepared for her.

How to Discern Your Gifting

Over the years, I have read hundreds of call stories from my students. Each is inspiring and marvelous. No two are the same. In one way or another, each student has had a divine encounter that has propelled him or her into some specific ministry. Having a calling motivates Christians to do the improbable and attempt the impossible. Recently, I saw this when an empty nest couple sold everything and moved to a remote place to translate the Bible into an indigenous language. Another student was a nuclear engineer who managed a shift at a nuclear power plant. During a missions class, God called him to go to Nepal. To gain access to the tribal peoples, he invented a portable solar water purification machine. Afterward, he mass produced them and distributed them to remote villages. Every few months, he returned to the villages to service the units. This became the basis of his evangelistic ministry.

A widow friend felt great joy when she discovered that she was a prayer warrior. Afterward, she traveled to pray against demonic strongholds so that the work of evangelism could go forth without as much opposition. An elderly man discovered that he had a gift of healing. Afterward, he used his free time to pray for the infirmed in long-term care facilities and hospitals. Some of the healings were very dramatic. Of course, different seasons of life may have different callings. Raising godly children in the fear of the Lord is one of the most important callings. In short, no one is too old or too young to be gifted for ministry.

Flowing with Spiritual Gifts

In the New Testament, gifts and ministry callings were often imparted by the laying on of hands (see 1 Tim 5:22 and 2 Tim 1:6–7). Acts says that Paul and Barnabas appointed elders in each church that they planted after engaging in prayer and fasting to discern who God had chosen (14:23). Unfortunately, most people don't have easy access to a New Testament apostle. Sometimes people come to me because they want to discover their calling or seek confirmation that they have properly perceived it. There are three primary ways to determine your calling and ministry gifts. First, identify your calling and then look for a spiritual gift mix that goes with it. Second, examine your gifting and look for the ministry calling that goes with it. Lastly, get a word from God through a vision, prophesy, or some other supernatural means. I prefer the third method of discerning your calling because it leaves little doubt and it has strong biblical precedent.

I felt called to preach when I was fourteen. In high school, friends called me Billy Graham because I was very animated about my faith. When I was eighteen, I laid a fleece before God. I told him that I would accept my calling to preach if he confirmed it that night at church. My fleece was very specific. Thankfully, God is a loving father who doesn't tire of the innocent antics of his children. During the evening service, Pastor Venegas quizzically looked at me. She then stated that she had a word for me and that she couldn't continue until she gave it to me. You guessed it. She said, "God says that he has called you to preach."

I don't recommend using spiritual gift inventory tests for many reasons. First, the Bible doesn't model that approach. Second, the process is cognitive and may not include prayer, spiritual discernment, or the affirmation of others. Third, normally, the lists only include gifts that are mentioned in the New Testament. For example, Christians know that God calls and gifts people for music ministry. That isn't listed as a gift in the New Testament. What about the gift of writing poetry, painting, producing inspiring movies, or doing interpretive dance? Certainly, Christians are called and gifted for these important ministries. For some, farming is a holy calling for which one feels a great gifting. Spiritual counseling is also a gifting. Often it comes with wisdom and the discernment of spirits. The calling to intercessory prayer is one of my favorite gifts. I met one older person who claimed a gift of knitting afghans for premature babies and people in the nursing home. Like a prayer cloth, she anointed each blanket with prayer and oil in hopes that God would use it to bless the person who received it.

SECTION TWO: SPIRITUALLY EQUIPPED FOR ANOINTED MINISTRY

In sum, God calls every Christian into the Spirit-filled life. When he does, he gifts them for specific ministries. Often a person will have a gift mix that includes a cluster of related gifts. Through gifting, God equips the church to do his work. As such, spiritual gifting and calling go together. God gifts his children to do whatever he calls them to accomplish.

Section Three

Defeating Demons

7

Overcoming the Enemy When Demons Appear

PREVIOUS CHAPTERS HAVE DISCUSSED the importance of exorcism in the ministry of Jesus, the apostles, the seventy disciples, and the New Testament church in Acts. It is a sign of the kingdom and shows that Jesus has authority over Satan. As evidence that Jesus is stronger than Satan, he bound the strong man (Satan) and began to plunder his kingdom through exorcism (Luke 11:17–22) after winning a tactical battle with Satan during his temptation in the wilderness.

The Gospel of Mark graphically shows this point while Jesus was preaching his first sermon immediately after his temptation. "Just then a man in their synagogue who was possessed by an impure spirit cried out, 'What do you want with us, Jesus of Nazareth? Have you come to destroy us? I know who you are—the Holy One of God!' 'Be quiet!' said Jesus sternly. 'Come out of him!' The impure spirit shook the man violently and came out of him with a shriek. The people were all so amazed that they asked each other, 'What is this? A new teaching—and with authority! He even gives orders to impure spirits and they obey him.'" (Mark 1:21–27).

Throughout the Gospels, Jesus expelled demons from people. On one occasion, he let demons possess 2,000 pigs. Often, the demons yelled at Jesus or tried to make a deal with him. At times, Jesus talked to the demons before he cast them out. At other times, he shut them down and wouldn't let them speak. Jesus could vanquish a demon from a distance in the same way that he could heal from a distance. Even though Jesus focused his exorcisms on the lost sheep of the household of Israel, he could also cast demons out of Gentiles when he was outside the borders of Israel. Occasionally, the demons threw their victims down or made them convulse. Jesus didn't stop that. Luke 8:2 says that women from whom Jesus cast out demons followed him during his itineration. For example, he expelled seven demons from Mary Magdalene. The Gospels portray her as one of his closest disciples.

Jesus associated demons with unbelief, all manner of sickness, and being unable to speak. Luke tells the story of a woman that had been crippled by a demon for eighteen years. Jesus called her a daughter of Abraham who Satan had kept in bondage. Jesus walked up to her, declared that she was set free from her infirmity, and laid his hands on her. Immediately, she was healed (Luke 13:10–16). Anyone who casts out demons can cure a person who has a physical ailment caused or augmented by demons. In the Gospels, those include people who are deaf, dumb, crippled, stricken by pain, or have a high fever.

Demons Oppose Evangelism

Chapter 1 told the story of a demonized man who convulsed when I evangelized him. The spiritual environment surrounding evangelism isn't neutral. According to Paul, "The god of this age has blinded the minds of unbelievers, so that they cannot see the light of the gospel that displays the glory of Christ, who is the image of God" (2 Cor 4:4). Sharing the word of God shines light into the darkness of unbelief and is the chief means by which God removes the satanic veil that keeps people ignorant of God (2 Cor 4:5–6). Evangelists know that their work is resisted by demons. The demonic pushback may be visible or subtle. It can stymie preaching and cause people not to feel conviction.

A couple of years ago, I attended a service in which a gifted African American woman preached a dynamic service to a large church of progressively minded white people. Even though the message was riveting and the spiritual atmosphere tingled with Holy Spirit fire, a visitor kept disrupting the service with shouting. He wanted to divert the work of God. When the altar call went forth, the visitor continued to interrupt as Satan worked through him to stop the movement of God. The visiting minister ignored the ruckus and kept on task. Thankfully, the altar was filled with hungry souls.

Recently, I preached an evangelistic sermon on the Samaritan Woman story from John 4. While preaching, I felt the anointing and realized that God was doing something. As I prepared to give the altar call, a nonmember stood up, shouted out, and disrupted the service. I didn't hear what he said but I felt a dip in the spiritual temperature. It was an angry outburst because the Holy Spirit was stepping on his toes. Based on his behavior and its outcome, I would guess that the man was demonized. In any case, even though I gave a passionate altar call, no one came forward that day.

Luke 4:31–37 shows how anointed preaching can provoke the demonic. In that story, Jesus is preaching with kingdom authority. Those who understand the anointing know what this means. He isn't preaching like a rabbi who quotes from other authoritative sources. Rather, he is flowing in the Spirit. A spiritual power attends to his preaching. People sense God in his words.

As Jesus preached with the anointing, a demon became agitated and began to shout at him. "Go away! What do you want with us, Jesus of Nazareth? Have you come to destroy us? I know who you are—the Holy One of God!" (Luke 4:34). The man had many demons but it was the strongman who spoke. In this case, strongman refers to the strongest spirit that demonizes a person. Often, the strongman is the one who first came upon the person.

Upon encountering the demons, Jesus cast them out with a word. The demons were so overwhelmed by the living presence of God that they fled without injuring the man (Luke 4:35). Afterward, the people marveled because Jesus preached with authority and power. In this case, the text itself connects kingdom authority with spiritual power. In other words, when one ministers in the anointing, God's presence increases the person's spiritual authority and ability to do power ministry.

In his book on anointing, Benny Hinn writes, "The presence of God the Holy Spirit leads to the anointing of the Spirit, which is the Power of God, and the power of God brings forth the manifestation of the presence. The anointing itself—an anointing of the Holy Spirit—cannot be seen, but the power, its manifestations, its effects, can and should be seen. That is why I call it 'the tangible anointing.'"[1]

Recently, I read a popular book about a four-year-old boy (Colton Burpo) who visited heaven while he was in surgery.[2] While he was in

---

1. Hinn, *The Anointing*, 74.

2. I became interested in the topic of near-death-experiences while attending a conference on suicide prevention in 1998. In that conference, a leading researcher noted that people who survive a failed suicide attempt mostly have very dark or hellish near-death-experiences. Most recently, my thinking on near-death-experiences has been influenced by the research of Jeffery Long, MD. I recommend *Evidence of the Afterlife: The Science*

heaven, God showed him that he "throws down power" on his father when he tells Bible stories at church (preaches).[3] When the child told the story to his parents, he clarified that the Holy Spirit was the one who actually gave his father the power. From a four-year-old's perspective, anointing could be described as power from heaven.[4]

Two people can preach identical sermons. One may be technically trained but lack the calling and gifting to preach. The other may be equally trained. However, unlike the first, he is called to preach and gifted by God for that ministry. The sermon of the former may not bear much fruit. In contrast, the gifted preacher's sermon may produce a harvest of souls. Why? Anointing.

God is the power behind the preached word. The Spirit convicts, conveys faith, and draws people to Jesus. A gifted preacher who operates in the anointing will be a conduit through which God can do what only God can do. This is why seminary training without divine unction doesn't yield gifted preaching.

Let me add a word of caution. Just because a person is gifted and called for a ministry task doesn't mean that the person will always minister in the anointing. Sin, the cares of this world, demonic attacks, and fatigue can dampen the anointing in a person. Preachers should pray for the anointing before they enter the pulpit!

From a practical perspective, the anointed preaching of the gospel carries the power of God and may cause demons to manifest (Rom 1:16 and 1 Cor 1:18). Specifically, worship and anointed preaching weaken demonic influences in the surrounding environment as they energize a place with the power of God. That is why highly anointed services produce inspiring worship, miracles, and decisions for Christ.

Two years ago, a mother sent her eighteen-year-old daughter to my office for an intervention. When I conducted a routine oral history, I discovered that the woman had over thirty-five sex partners, did drugs, was sexually abused as a child, dabbled with the occult, and was an alcoholic. Since she had tried Alcoholics Anonymous, I suggested that Jesus could become her Higher Power.

---

of Near-Death Experiences, 2011 and *God and the Afterlife: The Groundbreaking New Evidence for God and Near-Death Experience*, 2017.

3. Burpo, *Heaven Is for Real*, 125–126.

4. For a scholarly discussion about anointing as it relates to New Testament word usage, consult Kendall, *Pigeon Religion*, 54–67.

OVERCOMING THE ENEMY WHEN DEMONS APPEAR

Once she decided that she wanted Jesus to become her Higher Power, I carefully shared the plan of salvation with her. When she seemed ready, I asked her to pray to receive Christ. She was eager to do so. Unfortunately, the demons weren't eager for her to accept Christ. When I started to pray, she felt nauseous, her chest began to hurt badly, and her head became dizzy. I didn't stop until her face contorted and she began to shake severely. I had run into a dead-end. She couldn't accept Christ until I dealt with the demons.

I arranged to meet her in my church's chapel. Before she left, I prepared her for deliverance with specific instructions. When we met the next day, I created a spiritually charged environment by sharing an anointed message about Jesus freeing the man with a legion of demons. Also, praise music played in the background. Two women assisted me; one took notes and the other gave a prayer covering. At some point, I anointed her with oil and prayed over the area. After I shared the gospel, I invited her to put her faith in Jesus. This time she received Jesus with outstretched arms and many tears. The demons couldn't prevent her from accepting Christ because they had been neutralized. Even still, the deliverance session wasn't a cakewalk. In addition to a prolonged demonic glower, her eyes rolled back, she had a silly half-grin, and a demonic voice mocked me. However, I reminded the enemy that the battle was already won at Calvary. Their resistance couldn't preclude the inevitable.

A few months back, I showed a Billy Graham video called *My Hope America*.[5] As the video played, the spiritual atmosphere became electrified with divine energy. My spiritual intuition told me that God was working. After showing the video, one young person wanted to receive Christ. After I shared the gospel with her, she seemed eager to go forward. When we prayed for her to receive Christ, she was stopped in her tracks by demonic manifestations. No amount of exhortation could break her free of her bondage.

While I was working with her, she confessed that she often felt pulled to Christ but couldn't receive him. Every time that she tried, her chest hurt and she became dizzy. This thought greatly distressed her. She feared that she couldn't become a Christian. Based on my experience with the anointing, I insisted that the gospel had the power to save her and that nothing could keep her from salvation if she would trust in Jesus.

I tried to share the gospel again. This time her head throbbed and she began to tremble all over. At that point, I realized that she couldn't receive

---

5. The Billy Graham Evangelistic Association. "Defining Moments." The site offers additional evangelistic videos that can be shown to individuals or groups.

Christ until I dealt with the blocking demons. After I cast them out, all the pain went away and she received Christ with much joy. She is still walking with him and is no longer in bondage.

Confronted by Angry Demons in Latin America

Two years ago, I preached a sermon in a Pentecostal church in Santa Ana, Costa Rica. Many confessed Christ or received prayer for healing. During the altar call, a mother came forward and asked me to bless her small child. When I prayed for him, the child began to hiss and growl at me. His little face was snarled and contorted. Instead of making a scene, I told the pastor that I wanted to see the mother and her child the next night at 5:00 pm. When they arrived, the child was beyond unmanageable. Five adults couldn't keep the child in order. While interviewing the distracted mother, I realized that she was the problem. I theorized that the child would be set free when the mother was freed. At a later point, I'll talk about soul-ties and how they work in a family unit.

The following night, five church leaders joined me for the event. They wanted to learn how to lead a person through inner healing. Because I was in Latin America, I would do everything in Spanish. I was a bit nervous about this since I like to quote Scriptures as the Lord brings them to me. Since I haven't memorized the Spanish Bible, I would have to translate the Scriptures from English to Spanish when I quoted them.

When the woman came in, I went over personal history. Her responses were typical. Before I started the ministry session, I wanted to ensure that she was a believer. If a person hasn't accepted Christ, I put-off deliverance until the person receives Christ. Otherwise, I will have to fight against stronger demons. In her case, as soon as I invited the woman to pray to Jesus, the demons took over. They yelled, "She can't say that name. She belongs to us." The demons shouted with such force that the leaders all fled. When they did, I was left alone with the demonized woman.

I tried to interview the demons to determine who they were, how they gained access to her, and what they had over her. In other words, what were their legal grounds for being in her? At one point, I told them to talk to me in English. They told me, "No." Evidently, demons don't have to speak English if the host doesn't know English. Frankly, I'm not positive that all demons know English. Possibly, they only know the languages that are spoken in the region to which they are assigned. Since they wouldn't cooperate, I told them to go down and not to interfere until I called on them.

When the demons went down, the bewildered woman looked at me with sad eyes. Tears streaked her face. She wanted to know what happened to her and why strange voices spoke through her. As we talked, I discovered that she was raped when she was eighteen by an uncle. At that moment, darkness descended upon her. In the last ten years, she had never said the name Jesus or prayed. Whenever she tried, the demons caused problems with her body. When I discovered this, I skipped everything else and started inner healing at the point of the rape.

With encouragement and prayer, she finally said Jesus' name. At first, it was forced and she didn't feel it. Soon, she was praying from her heart. In short order, she repented and received Jesus as her Savior with a lot of praise. As she did, Jesus gave her a vision of himself. His arms were reaching out to her and he radiated love for her. She couldn't describe his face because it was hidden behind intense light. Years of pain were released in a matter of minutes. Forgiving the rapist was hard. However, she was able to do that with Jesus' help. By the time we completed inner healing, she felt like a new person.

However, inner healing hadn't dislodged the strong demons. As soon as I began to cast them out, the woman collapsed and became unconscious. It is the demonic version of being slain in the Spirit. I call it the false death. I can't cast demons out when a person is unconscious. After fifteen minutes, the woman was cold to the touch and had shallow breathing. The demons had taken away my momentum and were controlling the outcome.

By this time, the five church leaders had returned and were urging me to call an ambulance. I didn't know how I would explain this to the police. Instead, God gave me a word. I told the leaders to surround the unconscious woman in a circle of praise music. I instructed them to sing until they brought heaven to earth. As they sang glorious praise, I spoke in the woman's ear. I explained that she was a child of God and that all the demons of hell couldn't prevent her from praising God. I also told her that the demons weren't allowed to go before the throne. As I described the heavenly surroundings, the praise reached a crescendo. At that moment, tears dripped from her closed eyes. Then her lips quivered as she tried to sing. Soon, she was standing with her arms stretched high. Praises flowed from her mouth. The fight was won.

Within fifteen minutes, I cast out forty demons. Unfortunately, these demons decided to exit through vomit. Normally, I don't allow vomit. I prefer deep sighs or yawns. I will accept coughing. I have heard burping and sneezing. In her case, I was just happy that they were coming out. Incredibly, her vomitus filled up five plastic bags. I estimate that she regurgitated two gallons of foul liquid. Humanly, that isn't possible. Yet, she did it.

During my follow-up visit with her, she told me that a handsome demon appeared to her when she was unconscious. He called himself Luzbel and said that he was a prince. He stood in the opening of a dark tunnel. He beckoned to her and asked her to give him her hand. She was pulled to the demon prince and wanted to respond to his offer. However, she resisted because she knew that he would destroy her. While talking to me about the vision, she kept saying how attractive he was. In her mind, demons were hideous and dreadful beings from which a person would flee.

More Demon Stories

A similar thing occurred last summer when I met with a politician from a large metropolitan center. The man wanted spiritual counseling to discern if he should run for re-election. He didn't like council meetings because the participants displayed a critical spirit. When he participated, he got painful stomach aches. I asked if we could pray about it.

The demons manifested as soon as we began to pray. They caused intense pain in his left forearm and his fingers. Before long, he was writhing and complaining of severe pain. His cries sounded like pleas for help. Since I hadn't started with inner healing, I didn't know much about these demons. After I began to rebuke them, they threw the man to the ground. His body became rigid. Drool dripped from his mouth. His face was badly contorted.

For some reason, the demons didn't obey my commands. In frustration, I stood over the man and began to repeat, "The Lord Jesus rebuke you!" With each command, I snapped my finger. Holy rage flowed through me. I was exceedingly angry that they were hurting this person. Every time that I moved my hand up and down with a strong snap of my fingers, I noticed that the man jerked. Soon, the demons went down.

After I got the man back in the chair, the demons returned and I began to reason with them. This may seem incredible to some. However, Jesus also "negotiated" with demons. They are sapient beings. As the demons glared at me through the victim's eyes, I told them about the coming judgment. In vivid details, I described their pending doom. I read from Revelation 22. I spoke about the lake of fire. The demons jerked the man repeatedly as I spoke. I reminded them that God will severely judge demons who harass his children. Finally, I asked them if they wanted to leave. With some urging, they acquiesced and released the man.

In the follow-up counseling, the man told me that he felt a whip every time that I snapped my fingers. He also informed me that the demons screamed when I snapped my fingers. To prove the point, he showed me marks on his body. Of course, none of that makes sense to me. I merely channeled God's rage and did the only thing I knew to do.

A Sleepy Demon

People often ask me how I know when a demon manifests. Mostly, it happens when I'm doing inner healing. At other times, they manifest when I am preaching or teaching. Last summer, I taught a spiritual warfare seminar to thirteen people over a five-day period. During the classes, I noticed that one of the participants always fell asleep when I got into my "preachy" mode. The man wasn't tired. He just fell asleep whenever the Holy Spirit charged the spiritual environment.

On Wednesday, the guy asked if I would do inner healing with him. When I went over his personal history form, I noted many possible groupings of demons. As I began the ministry session, three demons quickly manifested. They were anger, rage, and rejection. I knew who they were because they were angry and full of rage when they yelled at me. In fact, we got into an argument about which one was manifesting. When dealing with angry demons, you cannot become angry or you will empower them. If the manifesting demon is anger, I become serene and calm. When I cast them out, the man's eyes rolled back in his head, he made a loud noise, and fell backward on the couch.

When I told the person to sit-up, his head went down, his body went limp, and he went out. This wasn't the false death. It was sleep. I knew this was the sleep spirit because I had watched it all week. When I called the sleep spirit to attention, I asked it why it kept making the person sleep in the seminar. It responded, "I do not want him to hear what you are teaching. If he understands it, we will lose our control over him." I responded that I wanted the person to hear and understand everything I was teaching. With that, I cast it out.

Section Three: Defeating Demons

During the inner healing session, I cast out several other groupings of demons. Some left with a whimper. Others left in a more dramatic fashion by yelling, jerking, gaging, and causing the guy to fall backward. Each grouping was easily identified by its behavior. At times, I called out a grouping that I expected to find. At other times, a grouping appeared on its own. In short, demons often show who they are when they manifest.

Before I move on, I should say a word about the soporific (sleep) demon. It is a common spirit that often interferes with spirituality. I spoke about it in Chapter 2. Not only can it make a person feel very drowsy in church, it also makes people fall asleep when they pray or read the Bible. I know one woman who falls asleep every time she reads the Bible. Literally, she is asleep in two minutes. She cannot stop it and doesn't control it. She says that it feels like someone turns off the lights as soon as she tries to read.

At other times, a soporific spirit will make people drowsy when they drive. Besides being very dangerous, it is annoying. Some refer to this as driving hypnosis. When that spirit used to attack me, I would fall asleep at the wheel on a regular basis. Once it began, I couldn't force myself to stay awake. Many who have regularly suffered from this problem report that they can drive long distances without any sleepy feelings after they have been freed from the soporific spirit. It is a great joy to them.

Sometimes demons try to hurt the person who comes for inner healing. A week before writing this chapter, a professional music rapper came for help. He presented with agitation and anxiety. He wanted to be free. When we prayed together, no demons manifested. He accepted Jesus and told God that he desired to become a new person.

Afterward, inner healing revealed many demonic strongholds. For example, at five years old, he began to look at the porn magazines that his dad left out. To him, they were picture books. By six, he was stealing the magazines and reading them in the bathroom. From that moment, he was owned by lust. He stated that he hated lust and desperately wanted to be freed from it. However, nothing worked. He said that the perversion went to his core being.

As the session continued, he recounted the death of his dad when he was eleven. According to him, he refused to hug his dad the last time he saw him alive because he was mad at him. Later, drug dealers bludgeoned his father to death with a baseball bat. As he told me the story, rage and violence manifested. As he rapidly rocked back and forth, he pulled on his hair and beat his body with his arms. He screamed as he did.

At that point, I had to switch from inner healing to exorcism. When I did, the demons growled like a wild lion roaring. As I continued to cast them out, they screamed that fire was burning them. The entire time I cast them out, the man beat on himself, rocked in his chair, and made a growling noise.

I didn't complete the inner healing during my first session. Future meetings will deal with the other demonic strongholds. I did learn more about his story. Since drug dealers killed his dad, the man likes to beat up drug dealers. In turn, they have tried to kill him. Once, they unloaded many clips of bullets into his house. At times, violence takes over and he will do some randomly violent act. For example, something will come over him and he will kick the cat or punch something.

He also has a spirit of suicide that constantly speaks to his mind. After the drug dealers murdered his dad, he invited the suicide spirit into him because he cursed himself by saying that he wished he were dead. I couldn't let him go until I dealt with that problem. Afterward, I gave the man specific follow-up instructions.

In our follow-up conversations during the last two months, he has reported that he hasn't used any pornography and he hasn't become violent since our ministry intervention. At times, he feels an inward pull to his old ways. However, he has practiced warfare prayers when that happens. For example, last week his roommate kicked him out of the house for which he was paying half rent because he wanted to change things. Under normal circumstances, this would have caused a fight. This time, he just walked away and rented a hotel room.

His mother has also written me to tell me about the wonderful change that has taken place in her son's life. She said that she was liberated from her burden of fear because she is finally optimistic about her son's safety. Best of all, her son has started to compose inspiration rap. Some of the songs have already been recorded and played on radio stations.

A Spirit of Insanity

Sometimes, I receive calls from mental health counselors about a variety of issues. Three months ago, a counselor called to ask a question. She had a Wiccan patient. Whenever she talked with him, he told her what she was thinking. This freaked her out and made her paranoid. How was the guy reading her mind? The counselor wanted to know what to do about it. After I explained the problem, I suggested that her license wouldn't allow her to affect a good solution. I offered to meet with the client if he consented. He refused.

Soon after that, a different mental health counselor asked me if I would offer a spiritual intervention to one of her patients. The patient presented with anxiety, ritualized behavior, and spirit rape. Many mental health practitioners would have diagnosed her with paranoid schizophrenia. The counselor said that her spirit rape stories sounded credible and wanted to know if I could help her.

Before the patient consented to meet with me, she quizzed me about my knowledge of the demonic. She had very specific questions. Demonized people who see clinical mental health specialists learn to guard their words. They only reveal the deeper problem to people they trust. Often, mental health patients face negative consequences when they talk to their counselors about demons. A recent conversation that I had with a highly educated social worker about inner healing illustrates this point. She said that demons don't exist and that I should be charged with malpractice because I don't have a professional license to practice mental health. Furthermore, she didn't accept the premise that the practice of spiritual care allowed chaplains, pastors, and ordained clergy to deal with demonic issues. Fortunately, after the patient interviewed me, she was confident in my knowledge of the spirit realm and wanted to see me.

When I met with the woman, she reported that she suffered from frequent spirit rape. In her words, the main perpetrator brings other spirits. She can feel the demons. They make indentations on her body when they hold her down. Sometimes she has bruising. She also has injuries to her genitals. Medical doctors have documented the wounding. The problem has persisted for eighteen months. In her words, before the spirit rape began, she was a happy, well-adjusted, married woman who lived a very normal life.

The woman told me that she had frequent conversations with the head spirit. When it spoke to her mind, it communicated secret details about other people and future events. It talked to her while she was talking to me. Previously, it convinced her that it needed to be redeemed and she was the one who would provide him a means to salvation. He also threatened to harm other people if she didn't cooperate with him. She gave examples of harm that the demon did to others when she didn't obey him. In her mind, she was responsible for the welfare of those that the fiend threatened.

In response to the problem, the woman ritualized her life. She attended Mass every day, constantly prayed to many saints, and engaged in a plethora of folk practices that are common in folk Catholicism. For example, her rosary was always with her and she made use of holy items. On a frequent basis, she read written prayers at lightning speed. The rituals gave her comfort and made her feel some control. Even though she prayed to the Holy Mother and many saints, I noticed that she never prayed directly to God.

Before getting married, she said that she was a "sexaholic." Even though she had remained a virgin until she was twenty-four, she used a lot of pornography and had constant fantasies. When she started to have real sex, she went overboard. Sex controlled her life. Ironically, she married a man who was the opposite of her. Even though he was very affectionate, he didn't have an active libido. In her mind, he represented redemption. After marriage, she gave up pornography and resisted sexual fantasies. By choice, she became a sexually repressed wife.

At the end of our first session, I tried to discern the situation through prayer. As I prayed for her, the demons manifested with maniacal laughter and noisy chattering teeth. Every time I attempted to probe the demons, the crazy laughing became louder and more irritating. The chattering teeth reminded me of old people in an insane asylum. Both were very distracting.

Later I discovered that the crazy sounding laughter began after she had a sexual encounter with an older boy when she was six. She felt no shame and wanted more. The boy felt shame and refused to re-engage. Throughout her childhood and youth, she would break out in the uncontrollable laughter at odd times while in school or at church. It is a demonic counterfeit of the holy laugh. It distracts everyone.

I concluded my first session knowing that she presented with delusional behavior and that she was obsessive compulsive. I feared that she had traveled too far down the mentally ill road to be pulled back. However, I wanted to try to help her.

The above situation reminds me of a story that circulates in power ministry circles. An evangelist from the 1930s was walking along a river before a meeting. As he strolled along, he encountered a highly agitated man who was talking to himself. Recognizing the signs, he attempted to converse with him. When the man didn't respond, the minister said, "Sir, I perceive that demons are afflicting you. I would very much like to help you with that problem." The man merely groaned and looked detached. The exorcist continued, "I sense rage, anger, fear, and murder. Sir, can you feel them thrashing about in your chest? Do you mind if I speak to them?" Since the deranged man only moaned, he continued. "I am calling out to the strongman. Murder manifest yourself!" At that moment, the man pulled out a blade and stabbed the preacher in his upper arm. The moral of the story is clear. Don't call out the murder demon until you have disarmed him.

Before attempting an exorcism, I disarm demons by doing evangelism and inner healing. Inner healing discovers how the demons have gained access to the person, what legal claims they have on the person, and the means by which they remain attached to the person. Through inner healing, the deliverance minister helps the victim repent, forgive others, defuse curses, break harmful soul-ties, realize how the demons are attached, and eliminate their legal ground for being there. When this happens, a demon with a stronghold and a lot of power over the victim will become weakened. At that point, it can be more easily cast out.[6]

When speaking on this subject, Dr. Kraft muses that demons are like rats. They eat garbage. If your house is full of garbage, the rats will return as soon as you drive them out. In order to keep them out, you have to clean out the garbage. Inner healing helps to clean out the garbage on which the demons feed.[7]

Getting back to the story, in conjunction with her counselor, I determined a five-step treatment plan for the woman who complained about spirit rape. I also agreed to do inner healing at our next session if she didn't engage in ritual behavior to include constant prayers to the saints and use of folk Catholicism to control the demons. Also, she wasn't allowed to respond to the demons when they talked to her. When she felt threatened or stressed, she could pray to God. Additionally, I convinced her that the demons couldn't be redeemed; that she wasn't married to the strong one; and that she wasn't responsible for what happened to other people. Finally, she had to keep a journal in which she chronicled what she thought, did, and experienced between our sessions. She agreed to the plan.

She only contacted me one time during the intervening week to beg permission to use her prayer rituals. I declined and she abstained from

---

6. For those who want a deeper understanding of the inner healing process, I recommend Kraft, *Two Hours to Freedom: A Simple and Effective Model for Healing and Deliverance* and Wardle, *Wounded: How to Find Wholeness and Inner Healing in Christ.*

7. Kraft, *The Evangelical Guide to Spiritual Warfare*, 39–40.

them. Instead, I encouraged her to pray directly to God through our high priest, Jesus Christ.

When she returned for our next session, many demons were cast out. They gagged her and tried to make her vomit. Because I took charge, they didn't manifest with chattering teeth or crazy laughter. At the end of our inner healing session, the strongman presented himself. He argued that he didn't have to leave because he was married to her. I informed him that the woman never married him and that he manipulated her. After I broke his legal grounds for demonizing her, he told me how he came to her.

According to him, a year and a half ago, the woman was struggling with her repressed libido. Previously, demons had empowered it and used it as a tool to control her. She wanted to be free from it. To avoid arousing herself, she watched a G-rated family film. She ended up watching it over twenty times. She said that she watched it because it didn't include any sex themes and she liked the main character.

At some point, the incubus spirit appeared to her as the main character. He convinced her that he could help her with her marriage. By means of her interactions with him, she allowed him in. The demon attached himself to her sex problem and began to rape her. Eventually, the woman stopped fighting the demon and just accepted it. She confessed that the sex was great. She didn't believe that it was cheating because it wasn't with a real man. When he raped her, the demon had total control over her. Sometimes other demons assisted the main one.

When I cast out the strongman, the woman was radically changed. Even her facial features looked different. Most importantly, she had no symptoms of mental illness. She was a different person. In follow-up emails, she told me that she continued to reject all ritualized behavior, didn't hear voices in her head, reconnected with her husband, and had no more physical encounters with the demonic.

Both/And Thinking

When analyzing the relationship between the demonic and the psycho-biological parts of humans, Dr. Kraft teaches that people should think in terms of both/and instead of either/or.[8] For example, some physical illnesses can be caused or exacerbated by a demon. The same applies to mental illness. Some mentally ill people are also demonized. Others aren't. Mental illness

8. Kraft, *Defeating Dark Angels*, 85–93.

is an independent category that doesn't require demonization. However, most mentally ill people are harassed by demons because mental illness creates vulnerabilities and deep wounds that allow evil spirits to demonize them. Additionally, some demonized people appear to be mentally ill. They can be healed by inner healing.

Unfortunately, *the Diagnostic and Statistical Manual of Mental Disorders* doesn't allow for demonization.[9] Based on its commitment to an anti-supernatural bias, it believes that all human phenomena can be reduced to psychological, biological, and social causes. Spiritual causation doesn't exist even though mental health recognizes the importance of spirituality. For that reason, mental health providers don't recognize or treat demonization. Sadly, demons torment in full sight in mental institutions and no one can confront them.

If mental health allowed for demonization, the care of the mentally ill would be significantly improved. At the same time, many well-intentioned exorcists have hurt their cause when they have erroneously attributed all mental illness to demons. This ill-informed ideology is bolstered because some people who are classified as mentally ill respond to deliverance ministry.

Ministering in a mental institution can be a challenge. Often chaplains, pastors, and family members are restricted in what they can do. A former parishioner told me the following story about her close friend. The friend's sister was institutionalized for an unspecified reason. Every time the friend tried a spiritual intervention with her sister, she was rebuffed by the staff. Even anointed prayer cloths were returned to her. Finally, she got an idea. She knew that the purse checkers would allow her to give her sister an unopened bag of candy. Before she gave it to her, she took it to church, asked the pastor to put the bag in his pocket when he preached, and then asked him to anoint it with oil as they prayed together for her sister. At first, the pastor resisted. He relented when the sister explained her plan. After the friend's sister ate the candy, she began to improve and was finally released. The friend believes that God worked through the anointed candy.

A Muslim Comes to Faith in My Evangelism Class

Last year, a student came to class late because her arm became paralyzed and she couldn't drive well. After class, I offered to pray for it. Since she couldn't

---

9. American Psychiatric Association. *Diagnostic and Statistical Manual of Mental Disorders DSM-5.*

move her arm, she was eager to receive prayer. As I started to pray, I felt an intense heat in the arm joint. Soon the student had full range of motion. With great joy, she praised God as she raised her formerly paralyzed arm toward heaven. When her arm was fixed, the heat moved to her stomach and caused a lot of pain. At that point, we knew that it was a demon. As I continued prayer, the heat began to move to the throat. I expected that the woman would vomit. I commanded the demon not to make her vomit and to come out in a peaceful way. It obeyed. I knew that the demon left when the woman sighed deeply and yawned.

As she worshipped God and thanked him for his grace, God gave her the holy laughs. I have dealt with the demonic counterfeit. This woman had the real thing. She laughed for over ten minutes. When you hear the holy laugh, you want to laugh with the person. She was deeply blessed by the experience.

A few days later, a Muslim man from Saudi Arabia appeared in my evangelism class. When I arrived, he was talking to the students. He asked if he could attend my class. I sensed that God was up to something. However, I wasn't sure what was going on. I told the man that we talked about Jesus. I also told him that I didn't want to offend him. He assured me that he wanted to come to class.

I began the class with a devotional about the crippled man who was lowered through the roof by his four friends. I spoke about vicarious faith and healing through the forgiveness of sins. At this point, the visitor started waving his hand. When I called upon him, he offered an unanticipated reply. "Professor, I saw you do the same thing the other day when the woman was sick in the student lounge. You prayed for her and God healed her arm. Then you cast out her demons. How did you do that?"

By this time, my students were praying. The student closest to me was praying in tongues. In front of the students, I shared the gospel with the Saudi Arabian man. It was live evangelism. During the class break, he and I discussed what the Quran said about Jesus. After offering a Muslim friendly plan of salvation, I invited him to accept Jesus. The next day, two exchange students from Jordan showed up at my office door. They also wanted to talk with me about Jesus. On my Facebook page, I mused that the fish were jumping into the boat. How often does a Muslim from a closed country see a power encounter event, come to an evangelism class, and get evangelized?

Section Three: Defeating Demons

Stirring Up Demons through Anointed Preaching

Occasionally, when giving an anointed message, I sense that the demons are quietly manifesting in the people. I can feel it and see it in their body language. If you recall, anointed preaching and praise stir up demons. During the anointing, the demons may cause discomfort or try to get their host to leave. Sometimes, they will become so agitated that they scream out in the service or throw their victim to the ground. Often, this happened when Jesus preached. Since this presents a ministry opportunity, I like to flow with it. To be honest, at times I purposely cause the demons to stir in the people because I intuit that God wants to do something. Usually, this leads to inner healing sessions.

Recently, this happened when I was teaching on spiritual warfare. As I shared a devotional, I felt the power of God flowing through the room. I preached right at the demons without the students realizing what I was doing. I proclaimed the authority of Jesus and announced the gospel of the kingdom with faith. As I was ministering, I knew that the demons were moving. When the demons were sufficiently agitated, I asked how many were feeling stomach pains, nausea, chest discomfort, or constriction in their necks. Most responded in the affirmative. At that point, I shut the demons down because I don't like to do "group exorcisms."

One hurting participant couldn't make it through the rest of the day. I had to free him during lunch. After the session ended, two additional participants were set free. Others made appointments to be set free before the next meeting. If I hadn't flowed with the anointing and stirred up the demons, the people wouldn't have realized that they needed a spiritual intervention. Additionally, the manifestations became an object lesson that helped the students understand the content of the seminar.

Expect the Unexpected

Over the years, I have collected many demon stories. Most come from students who have taken my spiritual warfare class. During the class, students interview friends, relatives, and coworkers about their experiences with the supernatural. The following stories show that demons can physically manipulate a person. In a previous chapter, I related that a petite woman who was manifesting picked me up by the collar and pounded me against the wall. Those who minister deliverance know that they should expect the unexpected.

In the 1990s, a seminary professor traveled to Central or South America every summer. During a trip to Colombia, a distressed father approached him after he had completed an evangelistic sermon in a local church. The father convinced the professor to come to his home and help his young daughter who was badly demonized.

When they arrived, the father led the professor to an eight-year-old girl who was seated in the back corner of the dining room. She wore a pretty dress. Her legs were crossed and her hands rested on her lap. She was the picture of a sweet and innocent child. The duped professor knelt beside her and began to talk to her like any other little girl. Suddenly, the child turned toward him, peered into his eyes with the demon glare, and spoke with a deep and raspy voice. She said, "And who are you?"

Because he was not expecting that, the befuddled professor fell backward onto the ground. When he did, the demonized child roared with "otherworldly" laughter. After regaining his composure, the professor stood up and began to command the demon to come out of the girl in the name of Jesus. As the professor spoke, the demon continued to laugh with delight.

After a few minutes of laughing, the demon responded in its hellish voice by saying, "Is that all you have? Let me show you what I have." Then the demonized child stood up and walked over to a 200-pound solid oak table. With one hand, she grabbed a corner of the table, lifted it off the floor, and angled it vertically toward the ceiling. Realizing that he was in over his head, the professor left and returned with an experienced deliverance minister. The local exorcist was able to complete the job.[10]

In the late 1980s, a student at a Franciscan university in Steubenville, Ohio worked as a part-time custodian. One evening, Fr. Gus was in his office when she came to clean the building. Once the priest heard the student, he called to her and asked her to come to his office. Thinking that he wanted her to get his trash, she headed for his office. As she approached, Fr. Gus asked her if she was wearing her prayer armor. He recommended that she pray over herself before she entered the office.

When the curious student finally entered the office, she saw a young woman levitating about two feet off the ground. The woman was spitting

---

10. The story was shared by the Rev. Dr. Joe Stallings, a United Methodist pastor in North Carolina. He graduated from Ashland Theological Seminary.

and cursing. She called Fr. Gus all sorts of horrible names. She even threatened him with bodily harm.

Previously, the demonized woman had come to Fr. Gus to get help with some personal problems. Before starting the session, Fr. Gus prayed that God's holy angels would set a hedge of protection around them and their conversation. As he prayed, the demons manifested. When Fr. Gus told the demon to be quiet, the head demon said that Fr. Gus couldn't keep all of them busy at once. Fr. Gus confidently retorted that he was up to the challenge. That is when the woman started floating.

After the student entered the office, Fr. Gus continued to contemplate the problem. Finally, he said that he needed to go to the friary and get some backup. Before he left, he asked the student to manage the levitating woman. Specifically, he told the student to "Keep the dear woman safe."

The wide-eyed student stayed in the office with the floating woman for five to seven minutes. During that short time, the demonized woman called her names and started reminding her of past sins. The entire time, she floated off the ground. When three priests entered the office, the student left in a hurry.[11]

While doing ministry in the inner city, Dr. Petey Bellini met a thirty-year-old man who was deep into drugs and necromancy. The man said that he was a warlock and that he talked to the dead in graveyards. The dead gave him information that he wanted. Soon after meeting Petey, the man desired to be set free. As soon as Petey began to pray for him, the man flew backward and landed on his back. When he did, his eyes rolled back and turned red. He also began to growl and hiss in a demonic voice. Smoke began to come out of his eyes. As Petey continued the exorcism, the man started to levitate. Petey put all his weight on him in an effort to keep him low. Because of that, the man only levitated seven inches off the ground. While he was levitating, the demons continued to manifest. After an hour of spiritual warfare, the man regained consciousness and was delivered from the demons.[12]

George Otis also shares a remarkable story about levitation. In northern India, a young man became very ill. When the family determined that the medical professionals couldn't help, they sought the help of local Hindu

---

11. The story was shared by the Rev. Jean Coleman, a minister in the Lutheran Congregations in Missions for Christ. She pastors a Lutheran Church in Ohio. She graduated from Ashland Theological Seminary.

12. Dr. Petey Bellini is a professor of evangelization at United Theological Seminary in Dayton, Ohio.

monks. As the monks attempted to divine the cause of his illness through a ritual, one beat on a brass plate. Another sat before the boy in a lotus position. A third called on the local gods. Soon, the spirits possessed the sitting monk. When they did, the monk began to levitate six feet in the air. Within a few minutes, he began to fly in circles. As he did, the people began to cry, "god, god, god."

A local pastor was attracted to the banging sound. As he watched the flying monk and heard the people praising evil spirits, he began to rebuke the demons in Jesus' name. When he did, the flying monk abruptly fell to the ground. The crowd became upset because they were enjoying the supernatural entertainment. Upon witnessing the disruption, the head monk asked the pastor to leave. Even though the praying pastor had the power to disrupt the demonic manifestation, the pastor felt obliged to go because the people did not want Jesus.[13]

---

13. Otis, *The Twilight Labyrinth*, 26–27.

8

How the Demonic Manipulates Soul-Ties

THE LITERATURE ON SPIRITUAL warfare includes teaching on soul-ties. Per Terri Savelle Foy, a soul-tie is an emotional bond that unites a person with someone else. They are formed through close friendships, vows, commitments, promises, and physical intimacy. Harmful soul-ties are formed through abusive relationships (physically, sexually, emotionally, verbally), adulterous affairs, sex before marriage, obsessive entanglements with a problematic person, and controlling relationships. These types of soul-ties should be broken when doing deliverance for a person to find freedom.[1]

What Are Soul-Ties?

Derek Prince refers to "soulish ties." He explains that they characterize family relationships and close friendships. If one of the partners is demonized and/or abusive, the other can be controlled and manipulated by the person's demons through the tie. To show the danger of familial soul-ties, he quotes Jesus when he avers that a person's foes will be those in his own household (Matt 10:36).[2]

Charles Kraft defines a soul-tie as a relationship through which a person dominates another person. By means of unhealthy soul-ties, Satan brings people into captivity and keeps them locked into the bondage. In addition to family relationships and friendships, people form unhealthy

---

1. See Savelle, "4 Indicators of Wrong Soul Ties."
2. Prince, *They Shall Expel Demons*, 234.

soul-ties with people who dominate them emotionally, sexually, physically, and spiritually.[3]

David had a healthy soul-tie with Jonathan. "After David had finished talking with Saul, Jonathan became one in spirit with David, and he loved him as himself" (1 Sam 18:1). Some translations say that the soul of Jonathan was knit to the soul of David. They formed this soul-tie through friendship. On the other hand, David formed a bad soul-tie with Jonathan's father. Through it, King Saul pulled David into the unhealthy drama that characterized him and his family. The dysfunctional dynamics of Saul's family extended to David's first marriage. When Saul couldn't manipulate David, he tried to kill him.

The Mother/Child Soul-Tie

The most basic soul-tie is between a mother and her child. When a mother doesn't bond with her child, the child will become permanently scarred. Research has suggested a link between a mother's failure to bond and a baby's failure to thrive.[4] This environmental factor is associated with neglect and the absence of an emotional attachment. In fact, a baby needs a soul-tie with its mother. Usually, the bond is created in the womb months before the child is born. People who don't develop a soul-tie with their mothers at birth may cling inappropriately to other relationships or not be able to make close relationships later in life.

Most mothers who bond with their children can tell stories about empathetic links with their offspring. Some call it a sixth sense. Often, a mother can know how a child feels even when the child doesn't say a word. Some mothers can even sense a child's pain from a distance.

When I returned from a fourteen-month deployment after 9/11, a Marine Corps officer and I delivered a death notice to the parents of a lance corporal who was killed by a rocket-propelled grenade while serving in Iraq. After the parents greeted us at the door, the father said that they had been expecting us. They received the death notification with grace. Afterward, I asked them why they were expecting us since next-of-kin are never told about a military death until the Casualty Assistance Calls Officer makes an in-person notification. The father told me that the mother had a premonition when her son died two days ago. They knew he was dead and

---

3. Kraft, *Confronting Powerless Christianity*, 167.
4. National Institutes of Health, "Failure to Thrive."

had already dealt with the emotional pain before we arrived. They stayed home from work on that day because they expected that we would be coming with the official notification. I believe that the mother's soul-tie with her son allowed her to sense his death.

Recently, I heard another example of a "mother's intuition." A woman has a daughter who served as a missionary in the Dominican Republic. One day, the daughter had an unfortunate encounter with a local "witch doctor." During the confrontation, the shaman threatened her and threw something at her. The missionary ignored the person and went her way. When she left, the shaman cursed her.

That night, she became violently ill with severe pains. Soon her tongue swelled up and turned dark black. The missionary knew she was in trouble. On that same night, the mother woke from a sound sleep with a keen awareness that her daughter was in trouble. Since she couldn't call her daughter, she began to pray. The prayer burden was so intense that she prayed all night long. When the mother "prayed through to victory," the daughter was healed. In this case, the mother had spiritual standing to pray against the demonic attack because of her parental authority. The soul-tie enabled her to pray from a distance with effectiveness.

Manipulating Emotional Links

Some refer to soul-ties as empathy links or energy connections. Occultists and those who practice "alternative religions" often use this language. Advanced practitioners are called "empaths." In their literature, they form soul-ties with people via an exchange of strong emotions, rituals, or the provision of spiritual services like palm reading, psychic healing, or Reiki massage.[5] Through the empathetic ties, they can see into a person's soul, manipulate their life energy, and even feel their emotions from a distance. These practices open doors for demons and should be avoided.

Cult leaders like David Koresh of the Branch Davidians also create soul-ties with their followers so they can abuse them and keep them from leaving the sect. Koresh bound his followers to him through spiritual abuse, emotional dependence, false doctrine, and sex. For example, young girls went through a spiritual rite of initiation in which they had sex with him. He taught them to reject their biological fathers and to bond to him as

---

5. See Tedder, "What Energetic Connections Feel Like to an Empath." This article offers a superb explanation of how New Agers form, feel, and manipulate soul-ties.

How the Demonic Manipulates Soul-Ties

their true father. Since he was the Messiah, disobedience was sinful. He demanded absolute control over his followers. Other cult leaders have followed a similar pattern of manipulating soul-ties so that they can control followers.

Some years ago, I met a young woman who had survived many years of sex trafficking. At some point, she learned how to manipulate older men by forming emotional soul-ties with them. Quickly, the johns who wanted to abuse her became obsessed with her. When she broke free from the business, she continued to use her ability to attract older men, tie them to her, and manipulate the ensuing soul-ties so that she got what she needed. When she could no longer manage the web of entanglements, the authorities had to place her in a safe house for her protection.

During this time, a young Christian man befriended her. Although he never had sex with her, he developed a deep attachment to her. Whenever she had a financial need, he freely gave her money or bought things for her. Even though he believed that she played with his emotions, treated him badly, and wasn't as committed to him as he was to her, he couldn't live without her. He became so enthralled by her that his emotional state of mind revolved around the attention that she gave or withheld. Ultimately, he lost his job because he couldn't concentrate at work.

When he realized that a soul-tie bound him to the woman, he sought help from his pastor. Together, they broke the soul-tie. Afterward, he no longer felt tied to the woman. The change was dramatic. Without the spiritual intervention, the man would not have been able to extricate himself from this relationship.

The woman who survived sex-trafficking is a victim of Satan's malice and deserves to be set free. Thankfully, she went through a protracted period of inner healing and Christian counseling. With grace and time, God will recreate his image in her as he pulls up the deeply rooted tentacles of the enemy. In her case, soul-tie manipulation was a learned behavior and a demonically empowered gifting.

Recently, I gave pastoral counsel to a lonely woman who had formed a soul-tie with a business executive by repeatedly having sex with him. The man didn't love her or treat her well. Every time that she met with him, she felt used and bad about herself. Since she was a practicing Christian, she knew that her actions were wrong. Often, she told him that she never wanted to see him again. Still, she couldn't extricate herself from the soul-tie empowered relationship.

When she came to me for help, she repented and committed herself to purity. With her whole heart, she wanted to serve God and resist sin. Still, she couldn't flee from this caustic relationship. Time and time again she went to him in the middle of the night like a fish being reeled in on a fishing line. The problem didn't correct itself until she broke the soul-tie that bound her to him. After the soul-tie was severed, she told him how she felt, blocked him from her social media, and commanded him never to call her or text her again. Finally, she is free from him and his demons!

A few years ago, a pastor confided that he fell in love with a woman that he met on the internet. Every day, he talked to her, shared the details of his life with her, and exchanged intimate communications including pictures. Even though he had never touched this woman, he had created a very strong soul-tie with her. Obviously, the extramarital affair was destroying his marriage and killing his spirituality. Still, he lost his perspective. He wanted her more than his family or his own salvation. Literally, whenever he had a free moment, he opened an application on his phone so that he could connect with her.

Things finally came to a head when he told the woman that he wanted to meet her in person. The more he pushed to see her, the more he discovered about her. Ultimately, he found out that she had more than one online paramour and didn't want any guy to intrude on her real life or mess up her marriage. For her, online flirting was a hobby that kept her from being bored. When he realized that he had been played, he found the strength to break the soul-tie and move on with the life that God had given to him.

Forming Temporary Emotional Ties

Not all emotional ties are permanent. Some people connect for a short period while sharing something together. For example, during the Northeast blackout of 2003, elevators throughout New York City stopped working for five hours. A stranded college student reported on the group dynamics of the people in his elevator during the blackout. According to the student, of the five strangers on his elevator, one was highly claustrophobic. As soon as the elevator stopped working, she began to panic. The others immediately responded to her distress by distracting her. Since she liked classic rock, they sang every rock song that they knew. Soon, the mood in the elevator changed. The student reported that it felt like a family reunion as the people shared deeply personal stories and talked about life dreams.

After they got off the elevator, the students went their separate ways and returned to being strangers. In this case, the ability to form a quick and deep emotional bond with strangers served as a survival mechanism. However, when the crisis event went away, they no longer needed or wanted to maintain the emotional link.

While in ministry with hurting people, forming a temporary emotional "ministry link" lets a pastor enter into the other person's pain. Being fully present is a tenet of incarnational ministry and might be a spiritual gift associated with the provision of pastoral care. In the same way that Jesus enters into our pain and shares our suffering, pastors should enter into the hurt of others while doing ministry provided they maintain professional boundaries. When the ministry is completed and the pastor leaves, the link should dissolve. Ministers who don't maintain appropriate boundaries by letting go of the emotional link when they complete a ministry encounter may experience burnout or manipulate parishioners.

Recently, a very distraught pastor told me that he provided a quick ministry intervention with a female that needed some help. When he did, his pastoral heart caused him to care for her. To his chagrin, the emotionally starved woman misinterpreted his attention. Throughout her life, significant people had abused her and abandoned her. In the aftermath, her lonely heart clung to the pastor's emotional link and wouldn't let it go. She became obsessed with him. She stalked him, followed him on social media, talked to his friends, sent him gifts, and attempted to manipulate him into loving her.

Ultimately, he convinced her to undergo inner healing with me. When she told me her story, great tears flowed from her eyes. She didn't want to hurt the pastor or his marriage. Sadly, she had a long history of "needing people" to show her love. That's why his emotional care triggered her obsessive response. At a deep level, his love connected with an emotional wound and became empowered by a demonic stronghold. In the aftermath of inner healing, she broke free from the obsession and was able to center herself on the love that Jesus had for her. Jesus became an extension of the ideal pastor/father who will always love her and never let her down.

Can Demons Move through Soul-Ties?

Evangelicals affirm that the teachings of Scripture and the example of Jesus are the ultimate authority for faith and practice. At the same time, they acknowledge that ministry providers often discover practices, techniques, and theories that enable ministry, are blessed of God, and don't contradict Scripture. For example, even though the Scriptures don't indicate that Jesus practiced inner healing, practitioners know that the results set people free from Satanic bondage and the principles on which it is based are derived from Scripture. As such, skeptics who don't do inner healing should adopt an open posture toward it. In like manner, experience has taught me to be open-minded when a credible power ministry practitioner affirms something about casting out demons if it doesn't counter an established truth of Scripture. In other words, one should investigate the claim before one dismisses it because the Holy Spirit may have taught the other person something that he or she needs to understand.

In 1998, an experienced deliverance minister told me that he always broke soul-ties before attempting an exorcism because demons could flow through them. He cautioned, if you don't break the unhealthy soul-ties, the person's demons may elude you by escaping through an established soul-tie to another person. Afterward, the demons will try to return by means of the soul-tie. Furthermore, since all illicit sexual intercourse produces soul-ties, demons can traverse between people who have had sexual relations with people to whom they aren't married. This also applies to sexual abuse, rape, and emotional affairs.

When I heard this, I rejected the idea that a soul-tie was an actual thing that linked people together in the spiritual realm. Additionally, I saw no evidence to support the notion that demons could move through soul-ties. From an observational perspective, I knew that duos who shared a deep bonding with each other were emotionally knit together. However, from my perspective, soul-tie language merely tried to capture the nature of that relationship and explain how it worked. In my thinking, a soul-tie was a psycho-social fact that could be observed and studied.

Since then, ministry encounters have caused me to reassess my thinking. Previously, I told a story about the teenage girl who couldn't accept Christ because the demons blocked her. She manifested with chest pain, a headache, dizziness, and shaking. After I cast out the blocking demons, she received Christ and all the symptoms vanished. Even though this teenager didn't have any external signs of deliverance, I knew that the demons left because of the radical change.

While I was working with the teenager, her mother waited in another room. She knew that her daughter was spiritually distraught and that the daughter and I went into my office so that she could receive Christ. Afterward, the mother came into my office and asked what had happened. I explained that her daughter had just received Christ and that she was a new believer. The girl beamed with joy.

The mother had a quizzical look on her face. She said that while we were praying, she had sharp chest pains and constriction in her throat. She felt that it was a spiritual attack. When she prayed over them, she began to burp loudly and continuously. The burping lasted until we finished the teenager's deliverance session.

I explained to the mother that we had to expel demons from her daughter so that she could accept Christ. When we did, I surmised that the demons traveled to the mother through a soul-tie. Because the agitated demons had nothing to attach to in the mother, she could cast them out with prayer in the same way that I cast out demons that try to latch on to me when I do deliverance.

I don't know if I answered correctly. However, based on observation and the soul-tie theory that I knew, it seemed like a logical conclusion. Otherwise, how does one explain the coincidence? One could suggest that my prayers over the daughter stirred up the mother's demons because she shared a soul-tie with the daughter. In other words, the mom burped up her own demons. The next anecdote addresses this possible interpretation.

Two years ago, a husband accompanied his wife when she came for inner healing. He didn't practice sin, wasn't inflicted with demons, and was emotionally healthy. I could tell that he loved God and his wife. He wanted to be present during her inner healing session so that he could provide a prayer covering and give emotional support. Throughout the session, he remained in silent prayer.

The ministry session uncovered many spiritual strongholds related to emotional wounds, victimization, and sin from the wife's premarital life. We broke them as we identified them. However, like the teenager in the previous example, the woman didn't have any physical reaction to the deliverance process. When it was over, she felt ten pounds lighter and said that God had removed her demons.

Unbeknownst to me, while I was working with the woman, the demons escaped to her husband. Afterward, he had chest pain and physical distress. I first realized this when I saw his grimaced face and noticed that his hand gripped his chest. Over the next forty-five minutes, he burped repeatedly as he expelled his wife's demons.

Section Three: Defeating Demons

Finally, I believe that an empathetic person who establishes an emotional link with another person during a deliverance session may be more vulnerable to demonic "spillage" than one who doesn't. I have personally experienced this. For example, if I cast out demons that manifest in a group or during an evangelism encounter, I never experience spillage. However, when I emotionally connect with a person during inner healing, I often have spillage.

The spillage problem has bothered me for many years. How do the demons get to me even though I pray a protective covering? Soul-tie theory suggests the answer. They seek to attach to me because I am an empathetic person who readily forms emotional links with the people with whom I do ministry.

Even if demons don't travel though soul-ties, the practice of breaking soul-ties is still warranted. The example of the man who felt an infatuation with the sex-trafficked woman demonstrates this. Breaking his soul-tie to her enabled his separation and subsequent healing. Those who come out of cults also testify to the value of breaking soul-ties. Unfortunately, there are times when a family member must break soul-ties with loved ones in order to find healing.

In summary, deliverance practitioners should help people break harmful soul-ties when doing inner healing. If the soul-tie involves illicit sex, I have the person confess the sin, renounce the sin, repent of the sin, cleanse the mind, and ask God to sever the soul-tie that the sin produced. A presession questionnaire should encourage the person undergoing deliverance to make a list of all the people with whom he or she has formed an illicit soul-tie. After praying over the names on the list, the client should destroy the list as a symbol of breaking the soul-ties. Obviously, the person should sever contact with former lovers and return items that they exchanged. For other types of soul-ties, the practitioner can lead the person through an authority prayer in which he renounces the relationship, rejects the soul-tie, and claims the covering of Jesus.[6]

---

6. Doris Wagner includes several prayers for the breaking of soul-ties and a pre-deliverance questionnaire. See *How to Cast Out Demons*, 88.

9

Secondhand Smoke

WHEN I WAS A child, my parents smoked in the house. Since we didn't open the windows during the cold months, the smoke became thick before spring. When a ray of sunlight shone through the windows, the inside air looked like a yellow fog. Even though I didn't smoke, my parent's smoke entered my lungs and adversely affected my health. Similarly, when a person channels demonic behavior in the home, the behavior will affect the entire family unit. The following example illustrates this point.

Joan's Story

As a teenager and young adult, Joan survived two car accidents and many close calls while riding as a passenger with friends. After these harrowing experiences, she vowed to protect herself from bad drivers. Interestingly, she didn't react or feel anxious when she or her parents drove. However, she freaked when her husband drove even though he never had an accident. One of the most vivid memories of her honeymoon is the time that she jumped out of the car and began to walk away when her husband started to drive down a narrow mountain road that she considered unsafe.

When Joan's husband drove, a discernable behavior pattern soon emerged. First, she micromanaged everything in the car to include the radio, windows, and temperature control. Second, she told her husband when to turn, how fast to drive, which lane to be in, and when to stop. Since Joan was bad at directions, telling him when to turn caused problems. If he didn't execute a maneuver to her satisfaction, she criticized him. Third, whenever she saw a potential hazard, she told her husband to avoid it. For example, she yelled, "Don't hit that pedestrian" every time a person was anyplace close to the car. Fourth, trucks made her panic. She didn't allow her husband to pass them or be close to them because you can't trust a truck to stay in its lane. Fifth, if she tried to occupy herself by reading a book, inevitably she would look up and screeched, "Watch out" with fright in her voice. When she did, her husband would hit the breaks or veer wildly even though everything was fine. In her mind, her helpful warnings prevented many accidents. Her husband rejoined that her distractions and unnecessary screeches almost caused many accidents.

When first married, the husband tried to respond with understanding. At times, he would hold her hand and let her know that he was a good driver. Later, by mutual consent, he ignored her comments and refused to acknowledge them. That strategy failed. Finally, he mandated that Joan had to drive when they went out. Unfortunately, she didn't like to drive at night and couldn't drive the family's manual transmission. Plus, she thought that the husband should drive because her father always drove when the family went out together.

Whenever they drove together, the constant barrage of unsolicited advice, micromanaging, and dire warnings would eventually cause the husband to come unglued. When that happened, yelling became the norm. As expected, the children dreaded family car rides because they always included heated arguments that poisoned the atmosphere and ruined the trip.

Once, the oldest daughter invited a close friend to accompany the family on vacation to a distant city. The drive to the city was so bad that the friend called her parents and asked them to retrieve her before the vacation started. All were badly embarrassed when the girl's parents showed up the next day while they were enjoying the metro zoo. Since the girl had only interacted with the parents during home visits, she didn't realize how driving changed the family dynamics.

Over the years, Joan apologized a thousand times. Often, she promised not to act out in the car. However, she never succeeded. Finally, Joan admitted that she couldn't control her behavior. Even worse, when she allowed her fear, panic, and control to manipulate her husband in the car, the children got pulled into the fight. In short, because demons had attached to her past traumas, they could work through her to afflict the entire family when they drove. This is the "secondhand smoke" syndrome in spiritual warfare.

When Joan went through inner healing, she uncovered unresolved feelings from car crashes and stupid boyfriends who scared her by showing off when she was a passenger. She discovered how those emotional wounds triggered fear, anxiety, and control when she drove with her husband. In retrospect, she realized that she projected those feelings onto her husband. Furthermore, because of past encounters with guys of dubious character, Joan realized that she didn't trust men. Inner healing helped her heal those memories and free herself from the demons that had attached to them. However, it didn't deliver her from her habits and the patterned behavior that developed in response to the wounds.

I once heard Dr. Charles Kraft quip that it was easier to cast out demons than to change bad habits. When a student asked for clarification, he explained that habits associated with demonization are wired into the person. Sometimes a habit attracts the demon. At other times, the habit is formed in conjunction with the demon. Regardless of how bad habits take root in the individual, they don't go away when the demons are expelled. People who go through inner healing need to undo the offending habits if they want to achieve full freedom. That requires time and concerted effort. For that reason, Kraft urges people to see a Christian counselor after he completes inner healing with them.[1]

After going through inner healing, Joan knew that she had to cooperate with God to change her habitual behavior. At first, like a programmed auto-response, the old behavior continued to take over from time to time. When it did, she apologized, repented, and gave herself over to God. Over time, she improved. Then it happened. After a long weekend outing, the husband realized that his wife completed the entire trip without making one comment about his driving. More importantly, the family had an immensely enjoyable family getaway in which mom's anxiety didn't poison the air. Because of inner healing and Joan's determination to cooperate with God, the entire family was delivered from the consequences of her demons.

Soul-Ties and the Family Unit

Based on Joan's story and the content of the previous chapter, I want to share a theory about soul-ties and family units. Often, I encounter people with family curses that are passed down from one generation to the next.

---

1. For more information on this, see Kraft, *The Evangelical Guide to Spiritual Warfare*, 229–232.

Section Three: Defeating Demons

For example, a mother may have received a critical spirit from her mother. If not expelled, she will pass it down to one of her daughters. In one case, I traced a critical spirit back five generations. Recently, a man carefully showed me how he and his siblings had been vexed by generational curses that came to them through family soul-ties. Unfortunately, he had already passed the curse on to his children. His self-awareness came too late. However, he vowed to stop the curse in his new marriage.

Why does a generational curse stay in a family and how does it transfer from the parent to the child? To answer this question, we must realize that a family is a social unit in which the members share soul-ties. Furthermore, the social unit isn't one dimensional (synchronic). It is multigenerational (diachronic). The social unit includes the dead and the newly born. Within the family unit, the negative behavior of the parents and the resulting curse are passed down to the children through the demons that have attached to the family line because of the parents' sins. Simply stated, evil spirits that gain access to the family at a previous time stay in the family until cast out.

The evidence of the demon is the curse. The evidence of the curse is the patterned behavior that it elicits. Examples of generational curses are alcoholism, divorce, child abuse, anger, rebellion, suicide, poverty, and unfaithfulness. Some would attribute the multigenerational pattern to learned behavior, genetic predispositions, or environmental factors. However, the spiritual warfare practitioner has the added benefit of understanding how familial demons attach to family lines, exacerbate predispositions, and manipulate soul-ties. For that reason, whenever I see the evidence of generational curse (dysfunctional, multigenerational, patterned behavior), I look for the source.

Joan's story shows how her demons afflicted the entire family. Even if her husband hadn't been demonized before marrying Joan, his response to her would have created emotional wounds that enabled her demons to attach to him because her criticism and constant nagging made him feel anger, bitterness, and annoyance. In time, those emotions would color the relationship and bleed over to other social encounters. At some point, demons would attach to them and amplify the dysfunctional behavior. Eventually, the husband would fly off the handle, yell, and become very angry at the drop of a hat. The outcome is predictable when seen through the lens of soul-tie theory.

Since the children lived in the same house as Joan and her husband, the demonically empowered behavior would influence them. Mom's critical spirit and dad's anger would batter the kids over time. As they did, the children would become deeply wounded. When they internalized the dysfunctional behavior, they would react to it in ways that allowed demons to attach to them. They may become passive aggressive, disrespectful of authority figures, withdrawn, angry, or unable to bond to other people. After the demons had lodged in the children, they would be passed down to the grandchildren. At that point, a new generational curse would have been created.

Suppose that Joan's husband realized that he was demonized and decided to fix the problem. By means of inner healing, he would heal emotional wounds, forgive his wife, break strongholds, and free himself from the demons. However, as soon as he interacted with his family unit, the family demons would seek to revictimize him. How will he respond when Joan continues the behavior that caused the wounds that enabled his captivity? If he responds with anger, the demons will have an open door by which they can re-enter him. Even if the demons cannot re-enter the husband, they will harass him through Joan and the dysfunctional family dynamics.

Since demons work through soul-ties, the husband will have to do a lot of self-deliverance over the years to maintain his victory. I know this to be true because I do spiritual check-ups with family members who live with demonized family members. Also, he will need to change how he responds to the other family members. When seen from this perspective, it appears almost impossible for an individual who lives in a demon-infested home to remain free from demons. That is why I affirm that demonization is a social disease.

In most cases, family soul-ties serve a positive function and shouldn't be broken. Husband and wife, parent and child, grandparent and grandchild, and siblings are examples of God ordained relationships that are cemented with soul-ties. However, since demons attack family units and can move through soul-ties to demonize or harass other members of the family, the deliverance minister has a challenge. Even if he binds the demons in the person with whom he is working so that they can't move to another person when he casts them out, what is to keep the newly delivered person from being revictimized by the family demons that weren't cast out?

In response to this, I offer the following suggestion. In the same way that the church attempts to evangelize an entire family unit, it should attempt to cleanse the entire family unit from demons when individual members seek deliverance. In other words, without downplaying individual deliverance ministry, I am advocating for a family deliverance model. This gets to the social reality of demonization and helps to create a spiritual environment in the home that grows grace and produces spiritual fruit in the individual members.

10

Fire Ants and Demons
Knowing Our God-Given Dominion

IN 1999, AN OLD rodeo champion named Faye asked me to perform a funeral for an elderly friend who had died in another state. Faye was a strong woman and a mighty Christian. On the appointed day, we conducted the service at a funeral home. Next, we did a graveside burial. The graveside service normally takes fifteen minutes. I read a Scripture, give a short meditation, and offer the internment liturgy with concluding prayers.

When I started to read the ashes-to-ashes internment prayer, I felt something on my legs. When I looked down, I saw a small army of fire ants crawling on me. Soon, they would begin to bite. I concluded the service in lightning speed. Afterward, I dashed behind some parked cars. Faye was right behind me. With a loud voice, she said, "Preacher, what's wrong?" I cried, "Fire ants!" Together we battled the biting ants for five minutes. My pants were rolled up to my knees, and my shoes and socks lay scattered on the ground. Red bumps swelled wherever the nasty ants had bitten me. When we killed the last ant, Faye calmly suggested that I should pray against the fire ants. At the time, I had no clue what she meant.

Claiming Our Dominion

God gave humankind dominion over the animals (see Gen 1:28–30, 9:1–5, and Psalm 8). This fact is symbolized in Genesis 2:19–20, when God brought the animals to Adam so he could name them. In the ancient world, naming a child showed that the father had authority over it. According to God, animals must live in fear of people and are not allowed to harm them because they have authority over them. Even though the fall lessened humankind's dominion over the animals, it didn't nullify it.

Notwithstanding, human experience shows that some animals don't fear people. Anyone who has read about a shark attack, a snake bite, or a mauling knows that certain animals will hurt people. Even the Apostle Paul was bitten by a viper on the island of Malta (Acts 28:3). In his case, the venom had no power over him. Because the deadly snake wasn't able to hurt Paul, the Maltese people thought he was a god. This gave Paul an opportunity to evangelize them. In this instance, God protected Paul from the snake's poison.

My wife told me a remarkable story that illustrates this point. As she walked our Beagle through the neighborhood, a ferocious dog charged at her from a thicket. She said that it looked part Rottweiler and part Pitbull. Murder resounded in its bark. Immediately, fear filled my wife. Fear is her conditioned response to big dogs because a German Shepherd used to chase her when she rode her bike as a child. As if the barking and nipping at her legs weren't enough, when it finally bit her, her parents told her to raise her legs higher when it snapped at her. Because of this, she determined two things. One, she couldn't trust her parents to protect her. Two, big dogs pose a risk to one's safety.

On this day, a surging faith that welled up from within my wife canceled out her fear. With authority in her voice, she commanded the approaching dog to stop. Inexplicably, the menacing dog stopped in its tracks about five feet from her. In silence, the dog and my wife stared at each other. When my wife started to walk away, the dog began to come at her again. This time my wife claimed the blood of Jesus and told the dog that she walked under God's covering. With confidence, she commanded the dog to leave. Again, the dog stopped. This time it put its head down, turned around, and walked away. Even though the dog didn't understand the words that my wife spoke, it yielded to the authority that she exercised as a child of God.

In 2005, I attended a church planting conference in Orlando. During lunch, I found a secluded place under a sprawling oak tree to pray. I was deep in prayer when fire ants began to bite me. This time, I remembered Faye's suggestion and I began to command the ants not to bite me. As I did, I felt a surge of faith. To my surprise, the ants stopped biting me. Even though some of the ants remained on my legs, I didn't allow my prayer time to be distracted by them. I concluded my lunch break in sweet communion with God.

After my time in Orlando, I began to think about this issue more carefully. I remembered that some colorful people in church history had commanded flies and other bothersome insects to leave them alone. I wondered if I really had the authority to command bugs. I was about to discover the answer to my pondering.

For many years my daughter played soccer at Buckeye Woods. While she practiced, I enjoyed running through the various trails. A dirt path encircles a large wetland area that teems with nesting birds. Another path goes along a flowing stream to Lake Chippewa. A concrete bicycle path meanders around picnic areas, athletic fields, farmlands, and fishing ponds. My favorite path is a two-and-a-half-mile loop that winds its way through a patch of dense woods. Unfortunately, every time I came to the trailhead of the bucolic loop, a swarm of biting insects descended on me. The stinging cloud stayed with me the entire time I ran in the woods. Other parents covered their exposed skin with insect repellant in a futile effort to protect themselves from the nipping bugs when they walked on this loop. When I used bug spray, my sweat caused it to sting my eyes.

One day as I entered the wooded trail for another painful run, the usual swarm of mosquitoes and biting flies descended on me. They struck at me like lightning bolts from a dark cloud. My hands flailed wildly as I tried to fight them off my bald head and exposed extremities. Suddenly, God inspired me with a thought. I remembered that the lions couldn't bite Daniel in the lion's den. I also remembered when I prayed away the fire ants in Orlando. With a swelling confidence in God, I began to claim my covering as I commanded the bugs to leave me alone.

When I claimed my position as a child of God and used kingdom authority to declare my victory, the flies stopped biting. The swarm followed me for the next twenty-five minutes, but I didn't receive another bite or swat at any bugs. I had a perfect covering as I went through the woods praising God for his love and care. After that, I prayed whenever I enter the woods and always had protection.

Two summers ago, I provided weekly worship services at Firelands Boy Scout camp close to Lake Erie. One of the services was conducted in a lean-to shelter that was located deep in the woods. Literally, when they constructed the rustic chapel, they built it in a carved out clearing in the middle of a thicket. The first week didn't go well because a swarm of biting insects harassed me as I led the service. The second week, I arrived thirty minutes early. When the bugs came for me, I prayed my covering prayer. After I prayed the prayer of covering, I could hear the buzzing bugs and could see the swarm but wasn't bitten. For the rest of the summer, I successfully prayed that prayer every week. At this point, I know for certain that God has given me the authority to pray away biting bugs.

The example of my wife shows that our dominion also extends to the larger animals. Some years back, I served as one of the national chaplains for Philmont Boy Scout Ranch in the lower Rockies. Because of a drought, hungry bears were threatening people. Locals reported that some fishermen had been mauled by them while in a stream. One afternoon, I hiked down from a mountain and was making my way along a river trail as I headed toward the other side of the reservation. As I turned a corner, a very large male bear stood on his hind legs and glared at me. His pelt was a light grey. He towered over me like a giant. My instincts told me to panic. Since I was alone and my backpack contained food, I figured that I could be in trouble. As I slowly backed away from the bear, I heard rustling behind me. When I looked over my shoulder, a smaller female bear came up from the river and was on the other side of me. I had no egress.

If they killed me I wanted someone to know which bears hurt me. So, I pulled out my camera and took pictures of them. As I did, a calm came over me and I felt the closeness of God. I began to claim my authority and to pray my covering. Then, I slowly walked past the big bear who blocked my path. I was so close that I could have touched him. He didn't hit me or make any aggressive moves toward me. I believe that God protected me.

When I have shared these stories with students and friends, I tell them to test what I say. To my satisfaction, a few who have followed my suggestions haven't been bitten when they entered bug infested woods. None have tried it with larger animals. I can't say that a prayer covering will protect everyone. I can say that it works for me and that it worked for my wife. Also, I am reminded that Jesus told his disciples that he gave them authority to trample on scorpions and snakes (Luke 10:19).

Walking under the Covering of God's Protection

Second Temple Jewish literature offers a wonderful story that explains the concept of spiritual covering. In the book of Judith, a vast army wants to attack the Jews. The Jews see the threat and turn to God in sackcloth and ashes. They undergo a deep repentance as they humble themselves before the Lord. By their own means, they cannot defeat this enemy. Still, they assume a defensive posture. They will not surrender.

When the enemy general hears about their resistance, he summons the leader of Ammon. After Achior recounts the history of the Jews, he offers the general a stunning conclusion. "So now, my master and lord, if there is any oversight in this people and they sin against their God and we find out their offense, then we can go up and defeat them. But if they are not a guilty nation, then let my lord pass them by; for their Lord and God will defend them, and we shall become the laughingstock of the whole world" (Jdt 5:20–21 NRSV).

This same theme is played out throughout the history of Israel. Whenever the people of God walked in the ways of the Lord and honored his covenant, God established his rule among them and protected them from their enemies. One can see this "divine" protection as the Hebrew children are rescued from Egypt and taken into the Promised Land. The Bible teaches that God fights for Israel when they submit to him (Exod 14:14, Deut 1:30, 3:21–23, 20:1–4, Josh 23:10, and Neh 4:20). However, when Israel sins, God removes his covering and lets her enemies destroy her. Long sections of prophetic literature make this case.

Thankfully, the Lord is a compassionate and gracious God who is slow to anger and abounds in love. He forgives wickedness, rebellion, and sin when the people return to him and repent (Exod 32:6). This allows him to reestablish his covering over the people.

God revealed this truth to King Solomon when he promised that judgment will give way to mercy when the people repent. "When I shut up the heavens so that there is no rain, or command locusts to devour the land or send a plague among my people, if my people, who are called by my name, will humble themselves and pray and seek my face and turn from their wicked ways, then I will hear from heaven, and I will forgive their sin and will heal their land" (2 Chr 7:13–14).

The same truth applies to families and other social units. For example, when the parents live in righteousness before God and each other, God's grace rests on the home. When the parents rebel against God and allow sin to dominate, the entire family unit suffers. This concept runs contrary to our egalitarian society that sees the individual as the basic social unit. America believes that children shouldn't suffer for the wrongs of their parents. Yet, everyone knows that they do suffer.

Section Three: Defeating Demons

Joshua 7 graphically illustrates how a person's sin influences a larger social unit. After God destroyed Jericho, Achan took some "devoted things" from the plunder and hid them in his tent. Later, when the Israelites tried to conquer the city of Ai with an overwhelming force, the people of Ai routed them. The defeat humiliated the Jews and tested their confidence in God. When Joshua took the problem to God, the Lord articulated a spiritual law. "Israel has sinned; they have violated my covenant, which I commanded them to keep. They have taken some of the devoted things; . . . That is why the Israelites cannot stand against their enemies" (Josh 7:11–12).

In truth, Israel didn't sin; one man did. However, because he belonged to a social unit called Israel, the entire people suffered for his sin. In the end, God decreed that Achan, his family, and all that he possessed had to be destroyed (Josh 7:25). Yes, the people stoned him and his family.[1]

The story of King Ahab and the Prophet Elijah also demonstrates the corporate nature of sin. When wicked King Ahab married Jezebel, a princess from Sidon, be began to worship the Ba'als, built a temple to them, constructed an Asherah pole, and gave the false prophets free reign in Israel (1 Kgs 16:30–33). To make matters worse, he persecuted God's prophets. To counter this evil, God sent Elijah to pronounce a judgment on the nation of Israel. The prophet declared that there would be neither rain nor dew for the next years.

When the drought became unbearable, God sent Elijah to challenge King Ahab and the false gods that he served to a dual. The power encounter took place before the people on Mount Carmel. In the competition, 850 false prophets build an altar and made a sacrifice to their god. Elijah also constructed an altar and made a sacrifice to Jehovah. According to the rules of the dual, whichever deity consumed the sacrifice with fire would be heralded the true God.

After the 850 false prophets made their sacrifice, they worshipped their gods from morning until evening. The worship included ecstatic

---

1. In a similar way, Adam's sin has predisposed his children to sin and has given Satan access to his progeny. The consequences of Adam's sin have been passed down to all people in spiritual and physical ways. Fortunately, God has determined to reverse this through Jesus Christ. First, God has adopted the saints into his family (Rom 8:17 and Eph 3:20). When this happens, God claims them as his children and cancels out the debt that keeps them in bondage to sin and Satan. Second, God is destroying the sinful image of Adam and replacing it with his own image. First Corinthians 15:49 declares this truth. "And just as we have borne the image of the earthly man, so shall we bear the image of the heavenly man" (NIV). In this way, the adopted children of God can break their tie to Adam's fall when they establish a new soul-tie with Jesus.

utterances, self-mutilation, and dancing. Their gods couldn't respond. Finally, Elijah called the people to him. When he declared that God was the true God, he prayed. At that moment, fire fell from heaven and consumed the sacrifice and the stone altar. Upon seeing this, the people fell before God and affirmed that God was the Lord. Afterward, the people killed all the false prophets. When they did this, God removed the curse he had placed upon the land. At the word of Elijah, the rains returned (1 Kgs 18).

When King Ahab gave himself and the nation to Ba'al worship, he acted on behalf of the people because he had authority to do so. Even though the people didn't ask for it, they were punished for the sin of their king. In some sense, his sin became their sin. On the other hand, when the people became convinced that Jehovah was the most powerful God, they killed the false prophets, gave their allegiance to God, and renewed their covenant with him. This act of rededication restored them to God. In conformity with the promise made in 1 Chronicles 7:13–14, God didn't destroy the people because they returned to him.

In a modern secular state that doesn't honor God or follow his precepts, citizen believers must hold the political powerbrokers liable for the evil that they allow. Sin invites God's judgment on the whole nation because abortion, sexual perversion, abuse of the poor, violence, pornography, divorce, and the like empower Satan's rule. National sins cause the righteous to suffer with the unrighteous because they all participate in the same political unit. Social transformation happens when the people turn to God and reorder their society so that God's precepts are reflected in the culture. To do this, the church shouldn't seek to create a political theocracy. Rather, it should seek to grow the kingdom of God so that God's influence reaches into all aspects of the society.

The concept of covering also extends to churches. People who unite to a church submit to the spiritual authority of the local church. A pastor is a spiritual gatekeeper. When the leadership team shepherds the people in righteousness, truth, love, and spiritual power, the people benefit from the spiritual covering that the pastoral leaders provide. Mere participation in the anointed ministries of a righteous church provides spiritual blessings to the members. However, when a church tolerates sin, error, and false religion, the church falls under the judgment of God and Satan gains access to the members. For that reason, the Bible mandates church discipline and requires that the people strive for holiness.

Section Three: Defeating Demons

Recently, three leaders of a large church sought my spiritual guidance because they and their fellow ministers endured constant spiritual attacks. In fact, except for the senior pastor, the entire leadership team suffered from strange illnesses, emotional abuse, marital problems, family issues, and spiritual malaise. Moreover, everyone who attempted to stand up to the manipulation of the senior pastor experienced unexpected hardships.

Through prayer and conversation, the leaders discerned a correlation between the injurious spiritual environment that had descended on the church and the leadership of the new senior pastor. The head pastor manifested a controlling spirit that came from insecurity and personal pride. His demeanor sucked the spiritual vitality out of the church. Worse, he let the demonic gain a foothold in the church. Before the senior pastor came to this church, it and its people thrived. Joy radiated from the people and their worship. Not only did the church prosper, its fame drew people from a large area.

In 2015, God led me to a wonderful house church of seventy-five people. The pastor worked as a lawyer by day and a pastor by night. She headed a committed ministry team. Most importantly, she didn't force the people to pay her the tithe. All the offerings went directly to ministry. I could tell that she didn't minister in order to receive. Because of her faithfulness, the people prospered under her spiritual umbrella.

When I returned to the church in 2016, I discovered that the pastor had become spiritually incapacitated because she blamed God when her son left the faith and her mother died. Because of her emotional pain, she stopped leading services and wouldn't provide spiritual leadership to the church. The attendance had dwindled. Anger, grief, and bitterness dominated her and the people.

During a special service that I was requested to lead, God gave an anointed message that touched the pastor's heart. She repented and renewed her relationship with God. Afterward, the people prayed over her and reinstalled her as their pastor. Subsequently, the power and blessings of God returned to the church and its members. When the spiritual leadership team walks with the Lord, the members walk under the covering that they provide.

Establishing a Covering

Saints need to establish a personal covering when Satan targets them with an assignment. When I was teaching at the biblical seminary in Medellin, Colombia during a sabbatical, one day I started to trip on everything. I stumbled over raised concrete, stairs, curbs, and objects on the ground. Literally, I feared for my life. Fortunately, I didn't break anything in any of my numerous falls. As a rule, I rarely trip or stumble on anything. Thirty years of playing soccer produced good balance and gave me an innate ability to walk without stumbling.

As I prayed over the problem, I received understanding. I was fighting against a demonic assignment. Perhaps someone had cursed me because they wanted to neutralize whatever God wanted to accomplish through me. Armed with that knowledge, I asked my host family to pray against my attacks. At the same time, I asked God to place his covering of protection over me. Immediately, I stopped tripping and stumbling.

The following week, while I was walking to the gym, God interrupted my singing to remind me to walk in his grace. Specifically, he told me that sin weakens his covering. Even when God desires to provide a covering, sin allows the demonic to gain access to his people. It is a spiritual law. If I want to walk in God's covering, I must walk in God's way.

This critical point goes all the way back to the Garden of Eden. When Adam and Eve sinned against God, they ceded their authority to Satan and compromised their relationship with God. To be sure, they didn't intentionally side with Satan in his rebellion against God. However, by means of their sin, they lost their covering and became vulnerable to Satan.

Throughout Scripture, God calls his people to live under his reign and reject the gods of this world. Idolatry is an obvious way by which people cast off God and align with demons. In the western church, biblical style idolatry is rare. Unfortunately, most don't know that all sin is rebellion against God and a means by which any person can fall under the influence and domination of a ruling demon. When one willfully violates the known will of God, the person walks in the stead way of Adam and gives himself to the evil to which he yields. That is why the saints must resist sin and submit to God. Those who practice sin won't inherit the kingdom of God, walk under his covering, or gain heaven (see 1 Cor 6:9-10, Gal 5:19-21, Eph 5:5, 1 Tim 1:9, Heb 12:14, and Rev 22:15).

When one sins, one becomes a slave to sin and to the power behind sin. When one lives for God and allows the Spirit of God to transform him from within, the person becomes the slave of God. Those who serve sin are under its curse. Those who serve God live under his blessing. God extends his covering to those who live as his righteous servants (Rom 6:15–18). Those who sin are delivered to Satan (1 Cor 5:5 and 1 Tim 1:20).

A Haunted Curve in the Trail

Earlier I noted that I enjoyed running through the bucolic loop at Buckeye Woods. One turn in the trail badly vexed me. No matter how carefully I stepped, I often stumbled when negotiating that curve. Fortunately, when I fell, I always escaped with minor injuries (scrapes and bruising). I would have been in trouble if I had broken a bone or twisted an ankle because the spot was far from help. To be clear, rocks and roots covered many parts of the trail. I always navigated them without tripping. I only struggled when running by one curve.

After completing a typical run in which I lost my balance at the curve, I asked myself why I always fell at the same spot. The coincidence was beyond chance. I concluded that something was causing me to trip. The next day, I slowed to a walk when I approached the turn in the trail. I noted that a prodigious tree protruded from the area. Its roots ran along the ground. The trail curved around the tree. I began to pray. Soon I was praying in the Spirit. When I finished, I spoke directly to whatever animated or haunted that spot. I told it that it couldn't cause me to stumble or hurt me. I prayed in the same way that I prayed in Colombia. As I prayed, I sensed God's anointing and felt that I had neutralized the problem. As I expected, I never stumbled, fell, or lost my balance in that spot after that time. Just to be careful, I usually, prayed as I approached the area.

Section Four

Spiritual Gifts Enable Spiritual Warfare

11

Dimensions of Healing

PREVIOUS CHAPTERS HAVE DEMONSTRATED that healing is a kingdom mandate. Jesus healed the sick, the apostles healed the sick, and the church is called to heal the sick. In fact, healing was so central to the in-breaking kingdom that Jesus commanded the disciples to heal the sick. In this age, he gives the church the ability to do divine healing because it reflects his grace and it pushes back the kingdom of Satan in a tangible way.

Healing is an aspect of spiritual warfare because Jesus associates sickness with the fall and the malice of Satan. Even though Adam and Eve were the ones who sinned, the fall is traced back to Satan's rebellion. He is the force behind it. He also sinned when he tempted Adam and Eve and when he rebelled against God. When the kingdom of God is fully realized and Satan is fully subdued, sickness will be destroyed. As the old preacher said, "Thy kingdom come, thy will be done, on earth as it is in heaven means that God wants to destroy sickness on earth because there ain't no sickness in heaven." Healing is a sign of the coming kingdom. Until the kingdom fully arrives, people will continue to get sick and die. No amount of healing will stop that. Still, every healing points to the consummation and is a means by which people celebrate God's victory over the darkness.

Thankfully, God has placed healers in the church. In the late 1980s, I pastored a church in Orlando. One of the older members was powerfully anointed to do physical healings. Usually, when a parishioner became sick or went to the hospital, they called Ralph before they called me. One woman had electrocuted her finger. By the time she finally went to the emergency room, the finger had turned dark black with gangrene. Ralph met the woman, pulled out his anointing oil, and prayed. When he did, the color flowed back into the woman's finger. She was fully healed. The hospital staff was amazed.

In the same way that God calls some to be missionaries, pastors, and teachers, he calls others to heal the sick. First Corinthians 12:28–30 establishes the office of healer in the local church. Few healers get released in ministry because insecure pastors feel threatened by highly gifted laity. Plus, most healers don't develop their gifting because they lack mentors and nurturing in ministry. Pastors and teachers receive formal training that equips them to walk in their calling. Who equips the healers?

Paul refers to the "gifts" of healing. Since the term is plural, one can assume that people who are gifted to do healing may not have the same gifting. There are many dimensions to healing. Some are gifted to heal muscular skeleton problems. Others have specialized gifting to heal cancer or some other physical problem. The more famous faith healers seem to heal everything.

Dr. Charles Kraft experimented with the gifts of healing during the signs and wonders classes at Fuller Seminary in the 1980s. He noted that he wasn't very good at physical healing. However, he was highly gifted at emotional healing. I love to watch him minister inner healing. He pulls demons out with the precision of a surgeon. Unlike me, he never gets excited or raises his voice. In fact, he is very gentle.

One doesn't have to have a gift of healing to pray for the sick. In truth, many people who aren't called to the office of healer discover that they can minister healing. Scripture shows that apostles, evangelists, missionaries, and elders often heal the sick. For instance, even though I don't claim a gift of healing, God has allowed me to heal a lot of people. As I previously noted, when I am ministering, God directs me to pray for people via hot hands and tingling fingers. By means of this, the Lord shows me where to pray. He always takes me to the right spot on the body.

A few weeks ago, a woman told me that she was suffering from a severe headache. Since I like to pray over headaches, I often ask permission to do so when I discover that a person is suffering from one. When I began to pray for her, I didn't feel anything in my hands. That concerned me because I have learned to depend on the feelings or anointing in my hands. Finally, I felt a little unction. When I finished, I wasn't expecting much. To my surprise, the woman was moved.

According to her, as I prayed, she saw a bright orange glow where my hand was hovering over her. She also felt intense heat on her side. When

I finished praying, the headache was completely gone. Needless to say, she was excited. From this experience, I have learned that I shouldn't put too much emphasis on what I feel in my hands. God tells the church that the prayer of faith will heal the sick (Jas 5:15). Occasionally obedience to the command to pray for the sick is all that one needs to release the grace of God. Fear that one won't succeed in healing prayer is a primary reason that people don't pray for the sick.

Demons that Cause Illness

The Gospels show that a peculiar relationship exists between healing the sick and casting out demons. One would expect that Jesus cast out demons with a word of command and healed the sick with anointed hands. Yet, he doesn't always follow that pattern. Sometimes he healed the demoniacs (Matt 4:24, 12:22, 15:22–28, 17:18). At other times, he rebuked the sickness (Mark 9:25 and Luke 4:39). In Mark 9:42, Jesus rebukes the evil spirit and heals the boy at the same time.

Luke 13:11 shows that demons can cause or be associated with a physical malady. In the text, Jesus says that a spirit of infirmity caused a woman to be crippled for eighteen years. Afterward, he healed her by telling her that she was set free from her spirit of infirmity. That isn't how most modern people think about sickness.

Earlier, I told the story of a woman who couldn't move her left shoulder. When I prayed over it, the shoulder was healed; however, the pain moved to her abdomen. Afterward, she was bent over in severe pain because the demons were hurting her stomach. When I cast out the demons, all of her physical pains went away and she was fully healed.

A similar thing happened a few months ago when I was ministering to a person who had a bad headache. When I prayed for the headache, the pain went to the stomach and caused her to become nauseated. The woman reported that she could feel the demon in her stomach before I cast it out. Actually, this is quite common when ministering deliverance. Often demons cause physical problems that resemble known physical ailments. When they are cast out, the physical problems disappear.

Two years ago, I was ministering before a large group of people over a three-month period. While teaching, I noticed that a woman always jerked when I said certain things about Jesus. Over time, her jerking became worse. She also had constant tremors. One night when everyone was leaving, I asked her if she wanted her body to shake. She told me that she couldn't stop it. She said that it was a normal side effect of her neurological medication. In other words, she owned the problem. Still, I asked her if we could pray over it.

When I sat in front of her, the shaking became more noticeable. Based on this, I surmised that demons were aggravating a physical problem. In a hushed voice, I commanded the demons to release her. Slowly, her body stopped shaking and the tremors went away. Finally, only her fingers trembled. I told her to pray over her fingers until they stopped. Before long, she had no symptoms. Six months after this, she was still free of symptoms. In this example, we affected a physical healing by casting out demons.

I don't doubt that the jerks may have been a normal side effect of her neurological medication. At the same time, I knew that demons had worsened the symptoms because I recognized the demons manifesting when she jerked at certain words when I spoke with spiritual authority. This case illustrates the both/and principle. The resulting problem was physical and spiritual. If I hadn't affected a spiritual intervention, changing her medication may have fixed the physical symptom.

Recently, a relative complained of a painful headache. Since her pulse was racing, she took her blood pressure. It was 170/120. Normally, this woman's blood pressure is 115/65. Her blood pressure qualified as malignant high blood pressure and needed to be treated in the emergency room. If left untreated, it could have caused organ damage. As such, the woman began to panic as she prepared to go to the hospital.

I suspected a spiritual problem for many reasons. One, it came on her quickly. Two, it fed into panic, fear, and anxiety. Three, she has never had this problem before. Four, she had been practicing breakthrough praying and was drawing close to God the night before this occurred.

With her permission, we settled down to prayer. Before we did, we cleared the air of anxiety and praised God. Then I commanded the headache to leave and prayed peace upon her. Immediately, the headache left and her vital signs returned to normal. A few days later, the demons tried to do the same thing again. This time, the woman knew what they were doing. After praising God, she commanded them to go and everything returned to normal.

The Evil Eye

A few years ago, a person who ministered in Guatemala shared a fascinating story with me. A native woman was saved from native syncretism when she joined a Baptist church. This woman greatly loved God and steadfastly refused to return to her animistic ways. One day, she fell victim to the evil eye. It is a type of curse that is communicated via a malevolent glare. Often it is related to envy. To avoid it, many cover their children, evade staring, don't make overt compliments about people's appearance, and keep from wearing anything that attracts attention. Most will wear something like an empowered amulet to ward off the evil eye curse. The evil eye problem affects people in parts of Asia, the Middle East, Africa, and Latin America.

The Baptist woman became very ill after she fell victim to the evil eye. Her stomach hurt so badly that she couldn't eat. Finally, she went to the medical doctors. After they examined her, they said that nothing was wrong with her physical body. They didn't say that the problem was psychosomatic or caused by stress. They didn't even give her pills for acid indigestion or tell her to change her diet. Rather, they suggested that she visit a folk healer. Visiting a folk healer is the usual method by which locals cure the evil eye. Since she was a Baptist, she couldn't do that.

When she talked to her American educated missionary pastor about her problem, he told her that the evil eye was a fairytale. He believed that there was an underlying medical problem that the doctors missed. As such, she was stuck between a rock and a hard place. She had a spiritual problem that the medical personnel couldn't heal. Her American pastor couldn't heal her because he didn't know how to help her. Furthermore, he didn't even believe in the evil eye. Plus, she couldn't go to the folk healer because she was a Baptist.

Finally, her daughter became impatient with her. In desperation, she found a local Pentecostal preacher and asked him to pray over her mom. He agreed. When he prayed for her, he understood that the evil eye curse attached to something specific. That attachment allowed the evil spirits to cause her physical pain. When he prayed over the woman, he broke the power of the curse and declared that the woman was healed through Jesus' name. As he cast out the harassing demons, the woman experienced complete healing. Afterward, her Baptist pastor became very angry with her because she had allowed a Pentecostal preacher to pray over her.

12

Using Words of Knowledge in Ministry

ONCE, WHILE I WAS teaching about the word of knowledge, a student who subscribed to the doctrine of cessationism (the idea that sign gifts ceased when the Bible was written) interrupted to inform his fellow students that getting a word of knowledge lacked biblical support. I retorted that cessationism lacked biblical support, yet he still believed it. I then explained that the Bible establishes a spiritual gift called the word of knowledge and that Jesus modeled it. However, the Bible doesn't tell us much about its operation. Therefore, the person who walks in the gift of knowledge is free to explore how the gift works.

Throughout this book, words of knowledge have been mentioned. The spiritual gift is a personal form of revelation that the Holy Spirit puts in the mind of a believer. For example, the person will know something without realizing why. It comes as an overwhelming awareness of some fact or truth. Sometimes it feels like a deep conviction. It is as if God downloads something into a person's consciousness.[1]

Jesus offers a clear example of the word of knowledge during his conversation with the Samaritan woman. In the middle of an evangelistic encounter, Jesus told the woman to go and get her husband. The woman answered that she didn't have a husband. Jesus replied, "You are right when you say you have no husband. The fact is, you have had five husbands, and the man you now have isn't your husband. What you have just said is quite

---

1. John Wimber describes how the word of knowledge works in *Power Healing*, 248–271. To see the word of knowledge in action go to Cook and Wimber, "How Words of Knowledge Come."

true" (John 4:17–18). The insight qualifies as a word of knowledge because it wasn't conveyed through human means.

The Zacchaeus story offers another example. Jesus is walking through the crowd-lined streets of Jericho. A diminutive man by the name of Zacchaeus wanted to see him. However, he couldn't push through the crowds. Out of desperation, he went ahead of Jesus and climbed a tree so that he could see Jesus when he passed. When Jesus approached him, he looked up at him and called him by name (Luke 19:5). If Jesus knew his name through divine inspiration, the information came as a word of knowledge.

Personal Examples

My first word of knowledge came right after I was Spirit-filled in 1978. While at a Dairy Queen in Orlando, I witnessed a man upbraiding his wife in an unflattering manner. In my opinion, he acted with malice and without love. As I watched him, anger grew in my soul. Then, God gave me a word for him. Without any external evidence, I looked at him and told him that he was a Pentecostal preacher from West Virginia. As I did, he stared at me. When he asked me how I knew, I told him that God didn't like his behavior and that his actions weren't becoming of a person with his calling. Stunned silence ensued. He knew that it was a word from God. Afterward, he became visibly convicted and thanked me for the message.

In 2004, my wife and I attended a week-long minister's conference in Lakeland, Florida. On Friday, I went to a Waffle House for lunch. While eating, a drunk-sounding homeless man talked loudly about the upcoming lottery drawing. While he spoke, the Lord impressed six numbers on my mind. I wrote them on two napkins. When the man got up to leave, I approached him and handed him one of the napkins. With determined encouragement, I told him that he should play those numbers. He gave me an incredulous look. I smiled and repeated my suggestion. By now, everyone was looking at me. In a loud voice, he said that he would buy a ticket and play the numbers right away.

The next morning, my wife and I passed a newspaper box as we walked to breakfast. I told her that I wanted to check the lottery numbers. She laughed and reminded me that we don't play the lottery. I ignored her chiding. I retrieved the napkin from my wallet and compared my numbers to the ones listed in the paper. I announced that I matched five of six numbers. Anyone who played my numbers would have won $6,745 under

Section Four: Spiritual Gifts Enable Spiritual Warfare

the "Match 5" rule. My wife became excited. She wanted to see my lottery ticket. I reminded her that we don't play the lottery and told her that God gave me the numbers so that I could share them with a homeless man. My travel schedule didn't permit me to return to the Waffle House that day. I hope the man received the gift that God intended for him and that the bystanders realized that God loves that homeless man.

Some years later, while waiting in line at a 7-Eleven, God gave me a word for the woman in front of me. She was dressed in casual clothes, looked a bit disheveled, and was buying cigarettes. When she turned around after making her purchase, I told her that she was a nurse who specialized in neurological orthopedics. Then, I waited for her response.

She looked at me with piercing eyes to see if she knew me. Then she asked me how I knew her specialty. When she realized that I was a stranger, she began to talk with me. She told me that her license had been suspended because she stole some meds from a medicine cart due to a pain pill addiction. The pain pill addiction came from a back injury. She got the back injury from lifting a heavy patient. In the ensuing conversation, she recommitted herself to Jesus and determined to reclaim her lost life. For several months, we corresponded via email as God allowed me to speak truth and healing into her life.

In the summer of 2003, I spent three weeks cloistered in a hotel room in North Carolina preparing for my upcoming spiritual warfare class in the fall. During this time, I practiced getting words of knowledge with the hotel staff. When I ventured out to eat, I had many evangelistic encounters with strangers when God opened a door for a spiritual conversation through a word of knowledge. Over time, I learned to receive words of knowledge on a regular basis.

Occasionally, God gives me a very specific word in order to correct a person. A year ago, God told me that a Korean minister was having an affair. More specifically, I felt a burning in my heart when I saw the person's picture and knew that he was having an affair. Since the person lived in Korea, I recounted the specifics of the affair via a private Facebook message. We were Facebook friends. I didn't know all the specifics until I began to write. As I typed, the information just came to me. My words nailed him and he felt immediate conviction because he knew that God was reaching out to him. Ironically, God sent a similar message by another person to the woman with whom he was cheating. When the couple compared notes, they both realized that God was not happy with their actions.

Soon after that, a woman wanted to know if she could stop by my office to say hi. Immediately I received a word from God for her. I wrote back, "You have unfinished business with a person and you need to work through it before you can move on." I knew that God gave me the word to set the agenda for our meeting.

When we met, she didn't say anything about the word that I gave to her. However, as she was catching me up on her life, she reminded me that her child had died a few years back. The pain still bit at her. Then, without warning, she blurted out a deep secret. A person in power who came to give her comfort abused her trust by making a move on her. She loved and trusted the person just like he was her own father. The betrayal opened emotional wounds and led her into a time of scathing darkness. Previously, she never told anyone about the occurrence.

As she recounted the episode, her eyes welled up with tears and agony gripped her face. Years of suffering were cracked open by her revelation. In the next thirty minutes, she was able to forgive the perpetrator, find peace with herself, and reclaim her identity in Christ. Upon retrospect, I doubt if she would have shared the traumatic event if God hadn't given me a word about it before she came.

A few weeks ago, I phoned my brother who lives 1,200 miles away because I felt a nudge to call him. I didn't know why I felt the nudge. When he answered the phone, I anticipated having a conversation with him. Instead, I didn't offer any greeting. Rather, I immediately asked him what movie he was going to see. I don't know why I asked him that question. It just came out when he answered the phone. I didn't give it any thought before I asked it. Yet, I knew he was going to see a movie and I felt I needed to ask the question.

He responding by saying, "What? Did you just ask what movie we were going to see? How did you know that we are walking out the door to see a movie?" Since my brother doesn't see many movies, he quizzed me more about the strange question. Finally, he suggested that the Spirit led me to ask the strange question. That allowed for a "God" conversation.

Sometimes God gives me a "for no obvious purpose" word of knowledge to teach me to trust the gift. Recently, it was twenty-eight degrees when I left the VA hospital in Cleveland. God told me that it would be nine degrees on my car thermometer when I pulled into my driveway. More precisely, in my mind, I saw a picture of my thermometer turning to nine when I got home. That seemed like an incredible drop. When I pulled off the interstate forty-five minutes later, I recalled the word and got excited.

By now it was fifteen degrees. Since I was only five miles from home, I wondered how God would make this happen. I felt so sure about the word that I told myself that I would bet $10,000 on it if I were a gambling man. As I turned onto my street, the temperature dropped to twelve degrees. Incredibly, as I pulled into my driveway, my car thermometer changed to nine.

Normally, a spiritual gift is paired with a ministry calling. I could argue that I have the gift of the word of knowledge to help me do evangelism. That makes sense. However, I get words of knowledge all the time. Often, they have nothing to do with evangelism.

Esperanza: The Day God Gave Me Hope

In early January 2017, God spoke the name Esperanza (Hope) to me. During the next week, the name rang around in my mind like a rubber ball bouncing back and forth against the metal bulkheads of a ship in rough seas. Whimsically, I told my wife that I wanted to name our next daughter Esperanza. She seemed perplexed and wanted to know why I liked that name. I told her that God kept speaking it to me. She laughed and told me that it would take more than hope for us to have another child.

A week later, while I was ministering to a person about spiritual discernment and overcoming evil in an online format, a Hispanic woman sent me an instant message. Without waiting for my reply, she began to pour out her story. For two long years, she had been trying to have a baby. With her whole heart, she believed that God wanted her to have a baby. To substantiate her belief, she told me that a woman had given her a word that God would give her the child that she desired in his time. In the meantime, she had to practice faith. Another woman had a vision of her with a child. Both words came unsolicited.

When she contacted me, she was losing her ability to believe because two years had elapsed since she received the first word. Doubt clouded out her faith. As I sensed the young woman's desperate yearning, I could hear the distant lamentation of young Hannah when she cried out to the Lord for a child. It is the cry of many women from many countries. God heard Hannah's heartfelt prayers and gave her Samuel (1 Sam 1:9–28). In the same way, he heard the prayers of Sarah and gave her Isaac (Gen 21) and he gave barren Elizabeth John the Baptist (Luke 1:5–25). In each of these cases, God destined the resultant child for his service.

Using Words of Knowledge in Ministry

To add to her misery, the woman's husband didn't want a child. His resolute opposition to having a baby was an emotional barrier that diminished her faith and caused her sadness. He rejected the idea because he believes that the world is very ugly. His morose thinking flows from his personal experience. In short, he thinks that a baby would endure a lot of suffering during its life and that life is not worth the pain.

I told the woman that her husband lacked hope (*la esperanza*). When a person lacks hope, he's not able to see or realize the vision that God has determined because everything looks dim and dark. His negative disposition prevents him from having faith. I reminded her that her faith was contagious and that she needed to find a way to share it with him. That is, she needed to help him enter her world of hope.

At this point, she told me why she messaged me. She wanted God to pick the name of her child so that she could begin to pray for the child in a personal way. She had pleaded with God for a name but wasn't able to hear anything. Silence rang in her ears. Previously, she heard me give a word while ministering in her church. It was a powerful event that God orchestrated. As she listened to the word and saw how it played out, her heart stirred within her. On this night, she was sure that God had given me a word for her. Finally, she asked, "Pastor, I believe that God has told you the name of my child? If so, please tell me the name!"

Dumbfounded, I told her that I hadn't received anything for her. In truth, I wasn't thinking about her before she interrupted me. I felt a little put upon by her question. Then, God screamed in my ear. "Tell her that I have picked the name Esperanza."

At that moment, everything clicked and I caught up with God. I typed "Last week, God spoke the name Esperanza to me. I can't get the name out of my head. I believe that the name is for you." When I wrote Esperanza, I felt a spiritual charge and a sweet release. I realized that it was for this moment that God had given me that name. He heard this woman's desperate prayers and had determined to answer her through me. For that reason, he put that name in my ear and arranged for us to message each other. It is also the reason that God spoke a Spanish name and not an English one.

Immediately the woman liked the name. Then she asked me what it meant in English. When I told her, she thought that God had given me the name Hope. After I explained that God had given me the Spanish version of the name, she was blown away. Her faith surged and she was able to return to a place of joy and expectation as she prayed for the day that God would bring Esperanza into her life.

As a further confirmation, after I shared the name, I stopped hearing it in my mind and lost all interest in it. I still think it's a pretty name. However, I don't feel an attachment to it. When I gave it away, God took it away from me.

Receiving Knowledge through Dreams and Visions

Sometimes the divine knowledge comes by way of a vision or dream. John Wimber offers an interesting example of this.[2] Once when he was traveling on a plane, God placed a banner across the face of a fellow passenger. It read, "Adulterer!" He was taken back by this. While he was looking at the word written on the fellow passenger, the man asked him why he was staring at him. At that moment, God gave him the name of the woman with whom he was cheating. When he spoke the name to the man and asked who she was, the man became ashen and desperately wanted to have a private conversation. The extended encounter led to his salvation.

Technically, Wimber didn't have a word of knowledge. He experienced a vision. The vision communicated a truth to him in the same way that a word of knowledge did. In this example, the word of knowledge worked in tandem with the vision so the work of evangelism could go forward. Even though Wimber's example seems exoteric and a bit unusual, it is very instructive. Truthfully, God gives his saints special knowledge in many ways so they can do his work. Words of knowledge, prophecies, visions, and dreams are some of the more common ways that God communicates special knowledge.

A few years ago, as I was reading the Bible and meditating, I had a lucid vision of a young white woman. As my vision continued, I saw a slightly overweight black woman with straightened long hair. She wore a greenish vest over a blouse. She looked right into my eyes. Then she told me to call the young white woman. Immediately, I saw the woman again. She was standing in a dark room. Her body was slightly bent over with her head resting on the palm of her hand. One leg was propped on a stool. Her elbow rested on that leg. In the vision, she was crying. Not only did I see the woman, I also felt her emotional pain.

---

2. Wimber, *Power Evangelism*, 74–76.

Using Words of Knowledge in Ministry

At another time, I was trying to figure out why a particular family was suffering from a series of spiritual problems. We had prayed with the family and anointed the house, but the problems continued. I had asked God to give me insight. I had none. Finally, God gave me a dream that helped to explain the problem.

In my dream, I was walking down a neighborhood sidewalk when a demon came out of a front door of a house. He looked like a dark ghoul or a black cloud of sorts. When he approached me, I asked him for his name. He told me he was David. I then asked him from whence he had come. He told me that he was attached to a twenty-two-year-old woman. Upon hearing that, I began to rebuke him in the name of Jesus. When I did, he fled from me. In hot pursuit, I chased him down the street until he came to a house. When he approached the house, the owner's daughter and two friends opened the door and let him in. Since they gave him permission to be in the house, I couldn't chase him out.

This dream was the clue that I needed to solve the problem with the family with whom I was working. To make a long story short, the older siblings had been big fans of the Harry Potter books. After they moved away, the parents realized that the books shouldn't be read by their youngest daughter until she became a teenager. At the time, she was ten. Unbeknownst to them, the older child had placed the entire book series in his sister's closet when he moved out. He assumed that his sister would want to read them someday and didn't want them to be lost in transit.

Upon seeing the banned books in her room every day, the daughter's appetite for the books grew. Finally, she could no longer resist the temptation. So she read the books at night while her parents were asleep. Actually, she pulled the comforter over her head, turned on a flashlight, and read the books in complete secrecy. Like the prophet who ate the scroll (Rev 10:8–11), the taste of the verboten books was sweet like honey in her mouth. However, it turned her stomach sour. In time, the forbidden fruit of sin caused the girl to feel awful. Finally, the visibly distraught girl told her father what she had done and asked him to punish her for her sin.

The parents wanted to laugh because the image of their young daughter staying up all night reading under her covers with a flashlight seemed comical. Yet, they knew that this provided a serious teaching moment. The Holy Spirit had convicted her of sin. They had to go along with it. In the aftermath, the child had a deep repentance and turned to God with tears and godly sorrow.

Section Four: Spiritual Gifts Enable Spiritual Warfare

Getting back to my dream; when I recounted the dream to the family, the parents surmised that their daughter had opened a door to a demon when she engaged in willful and blatant sin. Additionally, upon research, they discovered that some Christian leaders had strongly advised parents against letting their children read the Harry Potter series because of its depiction of the black arts.[3] Chapter 3 showed how my family experienced a demonic attack in our home when we watched *The Eagle* together. The same may be true when people read certain types of books.

The parents didn't know what part the two friends who also appeared in my dream played. They recounted that the daughter and her friends had watched the Harry Potter movies in the house. They also wondered if any of them had inadvertently done something else that might have given supernatural evil access to their home. Regardless, armed with the knowledge that God gave through my dream, they were able to repent in a specific way as we tried to cleanse the spiritual environment in the home.

---

3. See Elliot, "Harry Potter: Harmless Christian Novel or Doorway to the Occult?" and Matrisciana, "Harry Potter Witchcraft Repackaged."

13

Raising the Dead Is Spiritual Warfare

IN THIS BOOK, I have argued that the kingdom of God is the theological lens through which Christians should understand the church's calling to do power ministry. Not only did Jesus preach the good news of the in-breaking kingdom of God, he invited people into God's reign. To enter God's kingdom, one must reject Satan and follow Jesus in faith and holiness.[1]

Jesus showed the contours of the kingdom when he invited sinners to follow him, healed the sick, cast out demons, cleansed the lepers, and raised the dead. Each of the above aspects of Jesus' ministry upended aspects of Satan's kingdom. Additionally, Jesus equipped the disciples to do everything that he did during the time he itinerated with them (Matt 10:7–8). Moreover, he baptized the entire company of believers with the Holy Spirit on the Day of Pentecost. At that time, the whole church worked to dismantle Satan's rule and extend the kingdom of God. That is the apostolic mission of the church. When viewed in this light, spiritual warfare should be the main business of the church. That is, the modern church should do the signs that Jesus did because they point to God's reign, foreshadow the ultimate defeat of Satan, and set individual captives free.

Throughout the global church, healings, miracles, exorcisms, multiplication of food, and the like are commonplace events. Each gives witness to the kingdom and advances the work of God. However, few Americans

---

1. In *The Satanward View,* James Kallas shows that spiritual warfare is a primary concern of the New Testament. In *The Kingdom of God Is Spiritual Warfare*, David Kwadwo Okai brilliantly argues that spiritual warfare is central to the advancement of the kingdom of God. The most noted book on the spiritual warfare hermeneutic is Gregory Boyd's *God at War.*

have talked to a person who has been raised from the dead through the ministry of the church. Should Christians expect this "ultimate" sign of the in-breaking kingdom? If so, why don't people hear more about it?

Raising the Dead Is More Common than You Think

I have heard credible reports about people who have been raised from the dead. Mostly the reports come from India, Latin America, Indonesia, the Philippines, and Africa. Because of the remote context, the majority of the stories are never reported to the outside world. It is possible that God brings people back to life on a regular basis. In his book, *Miracles: The Credibility of The New Testament Accounts*, New Testament scholar Craig Keener offers a multitude of credible coming-back-to-life stories from all over the world including North America.[2] He offers so many trustworthy examples that he has to divide them between regions. The stories are confirmed by medical reports and eyewitnesses.

Obviously, the resurrection of Jesus is the greatest coming-back-to-life event of all time because no one else has been resurrected. Others have been resuscitated or brought back to mortal life. Besides Jesus, the Bible records eight separate incidents in which God resuscitated the dead through a prophet, an apostle, or Jesus (1 Kings 17:22, 2 Kings 4:34–35, 13:20–21, Luke 7:14–15, 8:52–56, John 11:38–44, Acts 9:40–41 and 20:9–20). In the same way that the Bible doesn't list all the miracles that Jesus did (John 20:30–31), one shouldn't assume that the eight resuscitation incidents mentioned by the Bible were the only occurrences in which people were raised from the dead. Instead, these are the ones that were recorded.

In addition to the above examples, Matthew 27:52–53 says that many holy ones rose from their graves after the resurrection of Jesus. They went into the city and presented themselves alive to many people. The Bible doesn't say what became of them. The story could be a metaphorical way to talk about the present reality of new life for all who have faith in Christ. The being-raised-back-to-life image is also used in Ezekiel's valley of dry bones vision (Ezek 37:1–14) and of the two witnesses in Revelation 11:7–14. Neither account needs to be read in a literal fashion.

The raising of Lazarus in John 11 should be read as a literal event. It illustrates how God uses signs and wonders to accomplish his work. When Jesus heard that his friend was very sick and on the brink of death,

---

2. Keener, "Blindness, Inability to Walk, Death, and Nature," 508–660.

he intentionally stayed away. He states that Lazarus's condition is a means by which God will get glory for himself and for his Son. That is, by raising Lazarus from the dead, Jesus will manifest his kingdom, bring glory to himself, defeat Satan, and grow his church.

After Lazarus had been dead for four full days, Jesus went to his tomb. Upon arriving, he encountered the mourners. In particular, Martha and Mary were profoundly distraught. More precisely, they were perturbed. They told Jesus that he could have saved Lazarus if he had been there. Personal experience taught them this because they had witnessed Jesus heal all manner of illness. Through the eyes of emotional pain, they felt betrayed and deeply hurt. After all, they were some of Jesus' closest friends. They cared for him and they thought that Jesus cherished them. The unspoken question jumps off the page. If you loved us, why did you let this happen? Why didn't you come and heal the man you loved before he died? Of course, suffering Christians of all ages have asked the same question countless times.

Why Do Bad Things Happen to Good People?

Theologians pose the question in a more nuanced way. They talk about theodicy and ask why God lets bad things happen to good people. Often, hapless Job looms large in their ruminating. He is a righteous man who loves God and serves him with integrity. God has made him rich. Yet, the Evil One wants to destroy him. Eventually, God allows Satan to bring calamity to Job's life so he can get glory for himself. In the end, Job is vindicated, Satan is humiliated, and God is exalted.

When seen from this perspective, there is a close parallel between Job's and Lazarus's stories. God allowed both events to happen so he could bring glory to himself. Even though this is entirely true, the line of reasoning misses the deeper issue because it fails to approach the problem of suffering through the lens of a loving Savior who agonizingly dies for the world so that he can redeem the world to himself. Jesus is a suffering Savior who shares our sorrow!

Before Jesus went to Bethany, he already knew that he was going to raise Lazarus back to life. If I had been Jesus, I would have told the grieving crowds to stop crying when I arrived at the tomb. After all, he was on the cusp of raising Lazarus from the dead. He knew that their sobs were about to be transformed into immitigable joy.

Jesus didn't do what I would have done. He didn't try to fix their emotional pain by telling them about heaven. He didn't say, "Stop crying and watch what I'm going to do." Instead, upon feeling the pain of those he loved, Jesus entered into their emotional hurt. The same pain that stabbed at his friends also pierced him. As a result, he wept bitterly. That is, he identified with their suffering and took their pain on himself. In no way did Jesus allow his foreknowledge to separate him from their excruciating suffering. When I think of this, I am so thankful that I serve a weeping God, a God who enters into my pain and allows himself to hurt with me even though he knows that he will wipe away all my tears and free me from all pain in eternity.

While speaking to Martha before Mary arrived, Jesus offered a unique perspective on resurrection and eternal life. He tells Martha that eternity is now. He is the resurrection and the life (John 11:24–25). New life already flows in the spiritual veins of those who walk with him and have faith in him. For believers, the resurrection is a *fait accompli*. When one internalizes this truth, one can walk in hope and have peace in the most challenging circumstances of life. That is, the saints can claim the resurrection power and the actuality that they are already eternal beings seated with Christ in the heavenlies (Eph 2:6). Death has no hold on them. It isn't the end. It is only the beginning. In Christ, believers are forever alive.

Joseph's Story

I met Joseph while teaching in Lagos, Nigeria. He is a soft-spoken, diminutive man. Joseph and his team have planted over one thousand churches around the Muslim world in Africa. This humble man of God defers attention and seems uncomfortable when people push him for personal details. He prefers to focus on God and his passion for Muslim evangelism.

While growing up, he attended both the mosque and the church in his village in Sierra Leone. At some point, he became a Christ follower. After that, he was shot through the lower pelvis area. When the bullet went through his body, it lodged in his wallet. Later, he almost died from cholera. As his life hung in the balance, he promised to do whatever God wanted him to do.

A strange set of circumstances that bear the unmistakable mark of divine providence jumpstarted his ministry some years back. According to Joseph, his motorbike broke down on the outskirts of a notorious Muslim village. The chief had burned down the last church and the Christians were either in hiding or had fled. While he tinkered with his motorbike wishing that it had broken down in another location, Joseph heard a loud commotion coming from the village. When he inquired, a person told him that the chief's wife had died. At that moment, God told Joseph to go to the wailing.

Upon arrival, he made his way through the throng of mourners and went up to the dead body. At once he began to pray for her healing. He prayed with faith because he sensed that God wanted to raise her from the dead. A friend asked him if he prayed quietly. He said that he prayed very loudly. In fact, he prayed for over an hour with no external evidence that anything was happening.

Prevailing Prayer

James 5:16 teaches that the effectual fervent prayer of a righteous person is very powerful. Sin disempowers prayer and worldly concerns dry up the prayers of the saints. However, the Lord answers the prayers of the righteous (1 Pet 3:7–12). Of course, Jacob wrestled with God all night long until he fought through to the blessing. He was so desperate that he had staying power. He wouldn't stop until God blessed him (Gen 32). It was a pivotal moment in his life and in the history of Israel.

In Luke 18:1–8 Jesus tells the parable of a widow who bombarded an unjust judge with her pleas for justice. Finally, he granted her request because her constant petitions wore him out. In the same way, Jesus contends that the Father will hear the prayers of his faithful ones who cry out to him day and night. In Daniel 10, a territorial spirit called the Prince of Persia obstructed Daniel's prayers for three weeks even though Daniel sought God in humility and righteousness. Because of his diligence in prayer, an archangel name Michael was able to break through with the answer to his prayer.

On many occasions, Jesus spent long hours in prayer (Mark 1:35, 6:46). Often, he withdrew to lonely places so that he could commune with the Father and discern his will (Luke 5:16). At times, he prayed through the night (Luke 6:12). While in the garden, he prayed with such pathos that his sweat became as drops of blood (Luke 22:44). According to Hebrews, during his life on earth, Jesus offered up prayers and petitions with fervent cries and tears (Heb 5:7).

The apostles were so committed to prayer that they didn't want to be distracted by pastoral care ministries (Acts 6:4). That is why they appointed seven deacons. After a time of intense persecution, the believers prayed with such determination that God shook the house in which they prayed (Acts 4:31). Paul urges the saints to pray always (Eph 6:8, Phil 4:6, Col 4:2, and 1 Thess 5:17). His personal life modeled his teaching on constant prayer. According to Paul, Epaphras, his helper always wrestled in prayer for the Colossian Church (Col 4:12). One wrestles in order to win. Epaphras prayed through to the victory.

Prevailing prayer is a rare thing in America because most American Christians have a very pragmatic attitude about prayer. They suppose that God hears their prayer the very first time they utter it. As such, they don't need to labor in prayer. Anything else qualifies as "vain repetitions" (Matt 6:7). Simply say your prayer, trust God, and leave the outcome with him.

To an extent, this is true. According to the Sermon on the Mount, prayer is not magic. People shouldn't think that they can manipulate God with prayers that don't align with his will. According to the epistle of James, people lack because they don't ask God. When they ask, they don't receive because they have impure motives. That is, they petition with greedy hearts (Jam 4:2–3). Additionally, Christians shouldn't make long prayers in order to gain personal recognition. Luke 20:46–47 warns against pretentious prayers. "Beware of the teachers of the law. They like to walk around in flowing robes and love to be greeted with respect in the marketplaces and have the most important seats in the synagogues and the places of honor at banquets. They devour widows' houses and for a show make lengthy prayers. These men will be punished most severely."

However, Jesus' cautionary words weren't given to praying Christians who seek to prevail in prayer. I am reminded of godly mothers who spend long hours praying for wayward children; or prayer warriors who diligently pray over cities to break spiritual strongholds; or pastors who daily plead for God to send a revival on their people. God hears these prayers and will honor them! In particular, when God calls the faithful to engage in strategic warfare prayer, they must be prepared to stay in prayer because it breaks down spiritual strongholds and weakens the spiritual powers of wickedness in high places (Eph 6:12). Every praying person knows this reality. In fact, by means of intercessory prayer, God has equipped the church to push back the kingdom of Satan.

The Outcome of Prevailing Prayer

Joseph prevailed in prayer. Even though the dead woman's hand was very cold and hard, he wouldn't stop praying or give into doubt. Considering that he was invoking the name of Jesus in the presence of people who hated Christians, this should have caused him concern. Yet, he remained undaunted. Finally, he noticed that warmth began to return to the cold hand. When that happened, Joseph became more excited and prayed with more fervor. Soon the woman opened her eyes and sat up. Afterward, mayhem broke out. The people attributed the miracle to Allah. They shouted, "Allahu akbar" (Allah is great).

Like most curious people, I asked Joseph to tell me the woman's side of the story. Specifically, I wanted to know what happened to her when she died and how did Joseph's prayer bring her back. He was intrigued by my question. He assured me that he had quizzed the woman about her death experience and was happy to share that with me. According to Joseph, as he prayed for the dead woman, she was already far along in her afterlife journey. She was on a long road packed with other people going in the same direction as she was traveling. However, angels met her and told her that she had to go back because Joseph's prayers were calling her to return.

Joseph's prayers were effective because he prayed in alignment with God's will, he released his faith, and he wouldn't stop until he got that for which he prayed. Consequently, God's work was accomplished. If Joseph had stopped praying after a few minutes, nothing would have happened. Fortunately, he prayed through to the victory.

Obviously, the chief was happy when his wife came back to life. However, he was also suspicious. He asked Joseph how he raised her back to life. Joseph pointed to Jesus. The chief feared that Joseph might have animated the body with a different spirit, a trickster spirit that would leave in the night. That is a practice associated with animistic religions and with tribal shamans. As such, the chief told Joseph that he had to spend the night in his house. If his wife died during the night, things wouldn't go well for him. Fortunately, the woman didn't die.

In the aftermath, the chief called all the leaders together. He said that he was born a Muslim and would remain one until he died. Then he reminded the leaders that neither Muhammed nor any of the historical figures in Islam had ever raised a person from the dead. Since Jesus saved his wife from death, anyone in the village including his wife, was free to become Christian. He wouldn't persecute them. Then he gave Joseph a schoolhouse that the Roman Catholics had built, told him that others needed to be healed, and sent his people to him.

God answered Joseph's ministry with many signs and wonders when they came to him. Subsequently, a new church was planted with seventy-five recently converted Muslims. Like the woman from the previous night, the church was brought back to life in a village that tried to kill Christianity.

When the Apostle Paul was shipwrecked on Malta, he healed the proconsul's father when he laid on his deathbed. Afterward, the rest of the sick on the island came and were cured by God through the name of Jesus (Acts 28:7–9). In similar fashion, after Joseph raised the wife of the Muslim chief, people from surrounding villages came to him. Soon, he was asked to bring his ministry to their villages. In time, a network of churches was planted and nurtured in Muslim strongholds.

Since meeting Joseph, he and I have remained prayer partners and email friends. Currently, he is making a dangerous evangelistic tour through some of the most repressive areas of the Muslim world. Yet, he goes with assurance and confidence. Like Paul, he follows God's direction and waits for God's guidance. Once he knows God's will, he seeks to align himself with it. Because of his remarkable faith, unquestioned obedience, and willingness to suffer deprivation along the journey, God honors him with ministry success and gives him spiritual power.

For example, recently he drove to a distant village in northern Nigeria on backroads late at night because God told him to go. At some point, rifle brandishing Muslim bandits stopped Joseph and his helpers. They forced them to stand in front of the van. Joseph and his team thought that they would be killed by the Boko Haram henchmen. While the militiamen were going through their belongings, the team prayed for mercy. Even though the brigands knew that they were Christians, they didn't bother them. For an unexplained reason, they told them to get in their van and go. That is Joseph's life. It is how the gospel spreads to remote areas of Africa.

Yes, Joseph embodies the apostolic calling of the church and his ministry bears the unmistakable marks of an apostle. The Holy Spirit flows through him like electricity flows through and an open circuit. For Joseph, spiritual warfare is second nature. Because of his deep intimacy with God, he has learned how to walk in the Spirit. He has also learned the language and terrain of the spiritual world.

Conclusion

This book has chronicled my journey from being a doubter to becoming a power ministry practitioner. Circumstances, scriptures, mentors, personal experiences, and God have combined to lead me away from skepticism. Truthfully, I wish that I had read this book twenty years ago because I needed someone to dismantle my disbelief by showing me that God intended the church to do power ministry. I hope that fellow Evangelicals will carefully consider the scriptural case that I have made for spiritual warfare and doing power ministry in today's church.

In closing, I am reminded of Peter's response to seeing Jesus walk on the water. Even though he was skeptical and a bit afraid, he wanted to walk on the water. He is an example to all of us who want to do what Jesus did. Jesus told the disciples that they would do greater things than he did. If we trust him, we will find the faith to step out of our comfort zone and into the world of power ministry. It is the way by which God will grow his kingdom and destroy the work of Satan. He wants your help!

Bibliography

American Psychiatric Association. *Diagnostic and Statistical Manual of Mental Disorders DSM-5*. Arlington, VA: American Psychiatric Association, 2013.
Billy Graham Evangelistic Association. "Defining Moments." *My Hope America*. https://myhope withbillygraham.org/programs/.
Boyd, Gregory. *God at War: The Bible & Spiritual Conflict*. Downers Grove, NJ: InterVarsity, 1997.
Burpo, Tim. *Heaven Is for Real, A Little Boy's Astonishing Story of His Trip to Heaven and Back*. Nashville: Thomas Nelson, 2016.
Cohen, Martin. *Paradigm Shift: How Expert Opinions Keep Changing on Life, the Universe, and Everything*. Exeter: Imprint Academic, 2015.
Cook, Blaine and John Wimber. "How Words of Knowledge Come." https://www.youtube.com/watch?v=dDFC6GtpYlE.
Crim, Keith R., et al. "Jihad." In *The Perennial Dictionary of World Religions*. San Francisco: Harper & Row, 1989. 381-82.
Davies, G. L. *Ghost Sex: The Violation*. Pembrokeshire, West Wales: Paranormal Chronicles, 2014.
"Demonic Alien Abduction Stopped by Calling on Jesus Name." *YouTube*. (November 2015). https://www.youtube.com/watch?v=QmNM_E3wt8c.
Dunn, Matthew. "12 Million Pages of Declassified CIA Files Now Online." *NewsComAu*. (January 2017). http://www.news.com.au/technology/science/12-million-pages-of-declassified-cia-files-are-now-available-online-for-everyone-to-view/news-story/dec42351b61 b6c5cebdd737064c61672.
Elliot, Belinda. "Harry Potter: Harmless Christian Novel or Doorway to the Occult?" *CBN*. http://www1.cbn.com/onlinediscipleship/harry-potter%3A-harmless-christian-novel-or-doorway-to-the-occult%3F.
Glenn, Stacia "Eerie Things Going on at Serial Killer's Childhood Home in Tacoma." *The News Tribune*. (May 2017). http://www.thenewstribune.com/news/local/article149008344.html.
Graham, Billy. *Peace with God, The Secret of Happiness*. Waco, TX: Word, 1953.
Green, Athlyn. "The Entity: True Story about a Woman Who Is Attacked by Invisible, Paranormal Forces." *Exemplore*. (October 2017). https://exemplore.com/paranormal/The-Entity-True-Story-About-A-Woman-Who-is-Attacked.

BIBLIOGRAPHY

Gumbel, Nicky. "Talk 11—How Can I Be Filled with the Holy Spirit?" London: *Alpha International*. https: //static1.squarespace.com/static/534bf831e4b0288e77e2964a/t/5 3a99345e4b0e0ea717a292e/1403622213821/Alpha+-+Script+-+Weekend+Talk+3+--+How+can+I+be+filled+with+the+Spirit-.pdf.

Hagee, John. *The Three Heavens: Angels, Demons, and What Lies Ahead*. Brentwood, TN: Worthy, 2015.

Hinn, Benny. *The Anointing*. Nashville, TN: Thomas Nelson, 1997.

Kallas, James. *The Satanward View: A Study in Pauline Theology*. Philadelphia, PA, Westminster, 1966.

Keener, Craig. "Blindness, Inability to Walk, Death, and Nature" In *Miracles: The Credibility of the New Testament Accounts*, 508–660. Vol. 1. Grand Rapids, MI: Baker Academic, 2011.

Kendall, R. T. *Pigeon Religion, Holy Spirit, Is That You?* Lake Mary, FL: Charisma House, 2016.

Kraft, Charles. *Confronting Powerless Christianity: Evangelicals and the Mission Dimension*. Grand Rapids, MI: Chosen, 2002.

———. *Defeating Dark Angels, Breaking Demonic Oppression in the Believer's Life*. Ventura, CA: Regal, 2011.

———. *The Evangelicals Guide to Spiritual Warfare: Scriptural Insights and Practical Instruction on Facing the Enemy*. Minneapolis, MN: Chosen, 2015.

———. *Power Encounter in Spiritual Warfare*. Eugene, OR: Wipf & Stock, 2017.

———. *Two Hours to Freedom: A Simple and Effective Model for Healing and Deliverance*. Grand Rapids, MI: Chosen, 2010.

Kraft, Charles H. and David M. DeBord. *The Rules of Engagement: Understanding the Principles that Govern the Spiritual Battles in Our Lives*. Eugene, OR: Wipf & Stock, 2000.

Lindsey, Hal. *The Late Great Planet Earth*. Grand Rapids, MI: Zondervan, 1970.

Long, Jeffery and Paul Perry. *Evidence of the Afterlife: The Science of Near-Death Experiences*. New York: HarperCollins, 2011.

———. *God and the Afterlife: The Groundbreaking New Evidence for God and Near-Death Experience*. New York: HarperCollins, 2017.

Matrisciana, Caryl. "Harry Potter Witchcraft Repackaged." *The BereanCall.org*. (May 2012). https:// www.youtube.com/watch?v=Bbge47MDKSU.

Murphy, Edward F. *The Handbook for Spiritual Warfare*. Nashville: T. Nelson, 2003.

National Institutes of Health. "Failure to Thrive." In *MedlinePlus Medical Encyclopedia*. (March 2016). https://medlineplus.gov/ency/article/000991.htm.

Okai, David Kwadwo. *The Kingdom of God Is Spiritual Warfare*. Fairfax, VA: Xulon, 2014.

Otis, George. *The Twilight Labyrinth: Why Does Spiritual Darkness Linger Where It Does?* Grand Rapids, MI: Chosen, 1997.

Payne, William P. "Folk Religion and the Pentecostal Surge in Latin America." *The Asbury Journal* 71, no. 1 (Spring 2016) 145-74. doi:10.7252/Journal.01.2016S.11.

Prince, Derek. *They Shall Expel Demons: What You Need to Know about Demons – Your Invisible Enemies*. Grand Rapids, MI: Chosen, 2003.

Riordan, Rick. *The Trials of Apollo: The Hidden Oracle*. New York: Disney, 2016.

Rommen, Edward, ed. *Spiritual Power and Missions, Raising the Issues*. Evangelical Missiological Society Series 3. Pasadena, CA: William Carey Library, 1995.

Saint Anthony Di Padua Da Montefalcione Society, Inc., "Who Is St. Anthony?" http://www.saint anthonysfeast.com/whois.html.

Bibliography

Savelle, Terri. "4 Indicators of Wrong Soul Ties." *Terri Savelle Foy Ministries*. (July 2012). http:// www.terri.com/4-indicators-of-wrong-soul-ties/.

Tedder, Lorna. "What Energetic Connections Feel Like to an Empath." *The Spiritual Eclectic*. (May 2014). http://www.thespiritualeclectic.com/2014/05/06/what-energetic-connections-feel-like-to-an-empath/.

Tolkien, John R. R. *The Fellowship of the Ring, Being the first Part of the Lord of the Rings*. Boston: Houghton Mifflin Harcourt, 2014.

Wagner, C. Peter and John Dawson. *Territorial Spirits: Practical Strategies for How to Crush the Enemy through Spiritual Warfare*. Shippensburg, PA: Destiny Image, 2012.

Wagner, Doris. *How to Cast Out Demons: A Guide to the Basics*. Ventura, CA: Renew, 2000.

Wardle, Terry. *Wounded: How to Find Wholeness and Inner Healing in Christ*. Siloam Springs, AK: Leafwood, 2005.

Wesley, John. "A Plain Account of Christian Perfection, as Believed and Taught by the Reverend Mr. John Wesley, from Year 1725 to the Year 1777." In *The Works of John Wesley*, 366–445. 3rd ed. Vol. 11. Grand Rapids, MI: Baker, 1991.

———. *The Haunting of Epworth Rectory: An Account of the Disturbances in My Father's House*. Monmouth: Oakmagic, 2003.

Wimber, John and Kevin Springer. *Power Evangelism*. Grand Rapids, MI: Chosen, 2014.

———. *Power Healing*. New York: HarperCollins, 1987.

www.ingramcontent.com/pod-product-compliance
Lightning Source LLC
Chambersburg PA
CBHW072146160426
43197CB00012B/2269